When Richard Dawkins came on my radio
to dispute the value of
I wanted him to debate it
ful and robust response
levelled today at Christia
provide it than Chris Sinki

Journalist and ho. ... .r Radio *Unbelievable* show
Surrey, England

After establishing the importance of wisdom and respect when answering those who question our faith, this book provides us with a helpful selection of thoughts and responses to a variety of topics, from items in the news, to the big questions of life.

Amy Orr-Ewing
UK Director, RZIM Zacharias Trust
Oxford, England

Chris Sinkinson has provided an excellent model of how to defend and promote the Christian faith in the light of contemporary popular challenges – direct, informed, crisp, Biblical, and all with a dash of humour! A great collection of apologetic snapshots that encourages us to use everyday opportunities to share the truth of the gospel.

Jonathan Lamb
Keswick Ministries
CEO and minister-at-large

Chris is prepared to take on any question about biblical Christianity. He does a thorough job of giving cogent answers in an easy to read and interesting way. He is a great contributor to *Evangelicals Now* and has a wonderful gift of building up Christians to be confident about their faith.

John Benton
Managing Editor
Evangelicals Now

Chris Sinkinson makes apologetics come alive in this enjoyable book. Easy to read and great to give to your friends.

Marcus Honeysett
Director of Training for Living Leadership and author of *Finding Joy*
Kent, England

An unapologetic apologetic that argues the case that the Christian faith is built on solid ground. Chris Sinkinson is a compelling communicator who tackles the sceptics with confidence and courtesy. This is a book that inspires and informs.

Ian Coffey
Director of Leadership Training, Moorlands College
Dorset, England

Backchat

Answering Christianity's Critics

CHRIS SINKINSON

Chris Sinkinson is lecturer in Old testament and Apologetics at Moorlands College, Christchurch, England and one of the pastors of Alderholt Chapel.

All author royalties from this book will go to supporting students at Moorlands College.

Copyright © Chris Sinkinson 2014

paperback ISBN 978-1-78191-406-9
epub ISBN 978-1-78191-448-9
Mobi ISBN 978-1-78191-451-9
10 9 8 7 6 5 4 3 2 1

Published in 2014
by
Christian Focus Publications Ltd.,
Geanies House, Fearn, Ross-shire,
IV20 1TW, Scotland, Great Britain

www.christianfocus.com

Cover design by Daniel van Straaten

Printed by
Bell and Bain, Glasgow

CONTENTS

INTRODUCTION

Christianity has long had a history of giving an answer back to her critics. This is sometimes called 'apologetics'. Rather than being meekly apologetic, the Christian is to be confident in putting forward their case and dealing with objections. Apologetics means 'giving a word back' – a little like 'backchat', but without the attitude!

When Peter encourages his readers to answer their critics, he reminds them to 'do this with gentleness and respect'.

> Always be prepared to give an answer to everyone who asks you to give the reason for the hope that you have. But do this with gentleness and respect. (1 Pet. 3:15)

Christians are not called to win arguments, but to win hearts, and part of that task is to present the faith in a way that is winsome and courteous to the critics.

For a number of years, I have had the privilege of writing a monthly column for the national newspaper *Evangelicals Now*. Under the title 'Unapologetic Apologetics', it has provided me with an opportunity to engage with items in the news or more general issues in the defence of the faith. In this volume, a number of those articles have been gathered together to make a collection that can be read cover to cover or simply dipped into as a theme catches the eye. This is not a textbook or a manual. These are snapshot replies or observations on aspects of Christian truth. I hope that you find them a balance of confidence and respect.

In practice, this balance can be hard to maintain. There can be a fine line between being bold and being abrasive. Sometimes we may think we have been polite while our hearer thought us rude. To find help with this aspect of apologetics, we could turn to that practical workbook of living, Proverbs. In this book we find some apparent contradictions. For example, we are told: 'Do not answer a fool according to his folly, or you yourself will be just like him' (Prov. 26:4). Good advice for a Christian in their witness: avoid bad-tempered debates that degenerate into vitriol. However, in the very next verse we read: 'Answer a fool according to his folly, or he will be wise in his own eyes' (Prov. 26:5). This, too, is good advice for a Christian. At times, a witty reply to a silly objection is the best response.

A young girl in an RE class was asked by her teacher to explain before sceptical classmates why she was a Christian. She said: 'Well, my mum is a Christian and my dad is a Christian. They brought me up to believe in Jesus. I guess that's why I am a Christian.' The teacher objected scornfully: 'That's a pathetic reason. What if your mum had been stupid and your dad had been stupid? What would you have been then?' The girl replied: 'Well, then I guess I would have been an atheist'. Such an anecdote follows the advice of Proverbs 26:5 but not Proverbs 26:4! It was appropriate in the heat of the moment, but not a model of respect!

Of course, these proverbs are not real contradictions. The very fact that they stand side by side in two verses of Scripture shows that the Hebrew copyists had no embarrassment in holding them together. They are two sides of a coin and reflect the fact that situations in life are not simple. We need to exercise wisdom in life as we share our faith with friends. The sincere question asked out of genuine interest deserves a different reply than the sarcastic remark made by a bitter

colleague. Proverbs reminds us that we have to make a judgment and do our best in each situation.

Peter's description of apologetics in 1 Peter 3:15 reminds
me to always err on the side of Proverbs 26:4 rather than 26:5.
Respect is better than ridicule. After all, the crude and shallow
complaints of many critics of Christianity do them no favours.
As a communicator, Richard Dawkins is no fool. He can also be
capable as a writer and has a great mind. But his manner and
venom do his case no favours. Marcus Brigstocke, a comedian
and outspoken atheist himself, has recently written on Richard
Dawkins's 'smugness'. He writes: 'Richard Dawkins says at the
beginning of his book, "I would like everyone who reads this, by
the time they put this book down, to be an atheist". Well, I was
an atheist when I started reading *The God Delusion*; by the time
I'd finished it I was an agnostic. I was going to read it again but
I worried I might turn into a fundamentalist Christian' (Marcus
Brigstocke, *God Collar*).

Even atheists can find Dawkins's manner unappealing. Sar-
casm, derision and scorn rarely help anyone's case. But a bit of
gentle humour and sharp wit can help a great deal. How do we
distinguish between the two? We should always remember we
are ambassadors for Christ. What representation of Jesus do
we give in our words, our manner and our demeanour? Mark
Twain reputedly said: 'Never argue with a fool; onlookers may
not be able to tell the difference.' I think King Solomon and
the Apostle Peter would have liked that advice.

So I hope you enjoy this collection of articles that attempt
to strike that right balance in putting forward the claims of
Christ in the midst of an often contradictory culture.

Part 1

Talk about the News

ONE

On the Discovery of Noah's Ark

In April 2010, a Hong Kong-based exploration team claimed to have discovered Noah's Ark, or at least several large wooden compartments, 13,000 feet above sea level on Mount Ararat. Carbon-dating of the wood was supposed to demonstrate it was 4,800 years old. The discovery was reported in the mainstream tabloid press.

Photographs from the interior of the wooden structure even showed a scattering of straw. Given our Christian concern for evidence and apologetics, should we have been first to promote this great news story? Absolutely not. In fact, there are good reasons for us to give these stories a wide berth. As far as apologetics is concerned, sensational claims can quickly become an 'own goal'.

The claim to have discovered Noah's Ark surfaces regularly in the popular press. It captures the imagination like no other story. There is something plausible about the idea of a wooden structure being revealed untouched in the melting snows of Mount Ararat.

However, there are some good biblical reasons for doubting the ark would be found. Would the fresh timber used really have survived so many years without rotting? Would such a valuable amount of worked timber not have been immediately recycled and put to good use in the post-flood world? As for videos and photographs of such pristine wooden stalls, straw included, surely the only animal we could smell would be a rat?

So, if this report is another hoax (to add to a long legacy of hoaxes regarding discoveries of the Ark), then does that put the biblical account into doubt? Only if we give too much credence to sensationalised claims. This is particularly regrettable for us when evangelicals have contributed so much to credible, mainstream biblical archaeology.

The serious work of evangelical Christians, like archaeologist Donald Wiseman (1918-2010), Professor of Assyriology, Alan Millard, and Egyptologist, Kenneth Kitchen, have all been respected in mainstream scholarship, while also providing robust grounds for trusting the biblical record. Of course, many of the discoveries that have been made do not seem so spectacular and might not make the pages of a red-top tabloid. But, for the honest sceptic or thoughtful enquirer, these evidences will be trustworthy and persuasive.

To take a relatively recent example, we need to understand just how cynical and sceptical some historians are of the biblical record. Among archaeologists and historians there are those called 'minimalists' who (unlike 'maximalists') claim that the stories of the Exodus and the united monarchy of Israel are much later legendary accounts with only minimal historical value. The minimalists imagine that Israel emerged when unrelated tribes gradually united in Canaan and wanted to invent a common history. King David is understood to be as historical for Israel as King Arthur is for Britain – a legendary figure embellished by later romantic notions.

Between 1993 and 1994, excavations at Dan, the northernmost city of the Israelites, discovered three fragments of a victory inscription. These were part of a very ancient Aramaic monument produced by enemies of the Israelites and probably broken up by the people of Dan. The fragments had been reused in the walls of the ninth-century city and that helped establish that they were very old. Archaeologists arrived at a date of approximately 850 B.C. for what became known as the Tel Dan Inscription or Stele.

The inscription makes reference to the 'house of David' and 'King of Israel'. It is the earliest direct reference to the dynasty of King David. Produced within a century of the life of King David and by his enemies, it provides direct evidence for this early period of Israel's history. Of course, those minimalist scholars sought alternative interpretations to avoid the implications. Claims appeared that the Hebrew consonants of the name David could be translated differently or that the inscription itself was a fake. These claims were given little time among mainstream historians and only served to highlight how important the discovery had been. King David and his royal dynasty could not be dismissed to the shadows of mythology.

Of course, a find like the Tel Dan Inscription is not quite as spectacular as the claim to have discovered Noah's Ark. But poorly researched and over-sensationalised discoveries do evangelical witness no favours. More significantly, apologetics is not really a tool for proving that the Bible is true. The Word of God is its own best evidence. What historical and archaeological studies can do is to demonstrate that there are good reasons to trust the record of the Bible. More than that, we can show alternative explanations are not at all plausible in the light of history. We should join the sceptics in being cautious about the more sensational claims; too often these are offered for a quick bite of publicity and contribute nothing to this long-term task of confirming the trustworthiness of the Bible.

TWO

Is this really the God Particle?

A 2012 announcement in the news generated some extraordinary claims. Possible sighting of the elusive 'God Particle' caused one scientist, Michio Kaku, to state on CNN that it 'takes us to the instant of creation itself'. Notorious atheist and Oxford University chemist Peter Atkins claimed on the BBC that its discovery was 'another nail in the coffin of religion'. Does this particle really have implications for faith in God? Is there reason for a Christian to be unsettled?

The particle is properly called a 'Higgs boson'. Its existence was predicted in 1964 by Professor Peter Higgs at Edinburgh University. Scientists assumed it must exist because it explained why matter has 'mass'. It is a bit like the way we predict the existence of all sorts of everyday things we cannot see. When a letter lands on the doormat, we assume the existence of a sender even if we do not know who they are. There are many phenomena in the universe that lead scientists to predict the existence of other things we cannot yet observe. We will hear more and more about 'Dark Matter' in the years to come. So the Higgs boson was simply a particle that is predicted to have briefly existed soon after the moment of creation.

To track down this particle, the 'Large Hadron Collider' was built in Switzerland. Costing about $10 billion, it is essentially an 18-mile circular, underground tunnel staffed by 3,000 people. The purpose of this vast machine is to simulate some conditions similar to those that existed soon after the Big Bang. This is done by accelerating hydrogen atoms close to the speed of light (that means traversing the tunnel at 11,000 times a second!), and then observing the energy released when atoms collide. Recent reports indicate that the Higgs boson particle has been observed. Of course, the particle only exists briefly, and then disappears, so it will be some time before most professionals will be willing to state categorically that it exists.

But let us be clear what the 'God particle' actually is. Its existence has been assumed for over forty years. It is part of the standard model for the Big Bang. It is a particle that explains why the universe has mass. It is a particle that existed during an early period after the Big Bang (creation). Its discovery gives confirmation to a lot of complex, theoretical physics. What is the God particle not? It is not an explanation of where the universe came from. It is not a new theory about the universe. It offers nothing that contradicts what we read in Genesis, or indeed anywhere in Scripture. In fact, the very name 'God particle' is a hopeless misnomer. Coined by experimental physicist Leon Lederman, it was intended as a humorous reference to the difficulty of observing it. Professor Higgs was not keen on the nickname but, unfortunately, it stuck. As a consequence, some scientists and media outlets with an eye on publicity and profit use it for headline-grabbing remarks about religion.

What should a Christian say in response to these headlines? Firstly, I think we should celebrate human achievement and discovery. The modern scientific world view is founded on the biblical principles of Reformation Europe. All truth is God's truth. Secondly, we should be aware that rarely are facts allowed to speak for themselves. Scientists are not unlike politicians in sometimes putting a spin on their claims. Some atheists betray their own materialistic agenda in putting such a spin on the discovery of the Higgs boson. The wild theological claims made by Peter Atkins do little for his credentials as a scholar. Thirdly, we should emphasise that a scientific description of how something works does not contradict the theological description of why God made it. Paul wrote that in Christ 'all things were created: things in heaven and on earth, visible and invisible, whether thrones or powers or rulers or authorities; all things have been created through him and for him.' (Col. 1:16) Does the Higgs boson exist? I will listen to the explanations of those brilliant scientists in Switzerland. But to ask who made the Higgs boson and why, I will turn to Scripture for an answer.

THREE

God is Dead (again)

The denial of the existence of the God of Christianity is nothing new – Bertrand Russell's collected essays and lectures, published as *Why I am not a Christian*, were written or delivered between 1927 and 1954. Earlier brash arguments against the God of the Bible had been offered by Voltaire (1694-1778) and Nietzsche (1844-1900).

So what is new about contemporary atheism? The term 'New Atheism' was coined by *Wired* magazine in 2006 as a way of identifying a new, militant, popular brand of unbelief. U.K.-based groups like the National Secular Society now seem tired and old-fashioned. So, like Tony Blair's British Labour Party of the 1990s, atheism has had a rebranding since the turn of the millennium. New Atheism holds to the traditional atheist family values, but the packaging is much fresher, youthful and vibrant. There is no new content being offered. What is new about this atheism is its populist, aggressive militancy. In the U.K., atheists launched a bus poster campaign to inform us that 'There Probably is No God.' This new breed of atheists are evangelists for their cause. Can we now look forward to a new atheist version of the popular Alpha Course? We already have a church for atheists in London.

The watershed moment is almost certainly 11 September 2001. The terrorist attacks on the World Trade Center, with their appalling consequences, were inspired by religion. Therefore, it is felt that religious belief must be attacked and condemned. Previous generations had their polite forms of atheism that simply wanted to keep religion at a distance. The new atheism is militant in its desire to attack, critique and ridicule religious belief in any form.

Those described as new atheists include popular writers Richard Dawkins, Philip Pullman, Sam Harris and the late Christopher Hitchens. The comedians Ricky Gervais, Bill Maher and Eddie Izzard also share the platform. The diversity of these characters ensures that the arguments against the existence of God find many channels, including sober TV documentaries, best-selling children's fiction and light-hearted comedies. These atheists are often crude and delight in what a previous generation called blasphemy. They are aware of the power of film, humour and literature to make a point and win hearts and minds.

Bill Maher, a popular American broadcaster, produced the comedy documentary *Religulous* in 2008 as an attempt to spoof, mock and undermine religious faith. Christianity is the main target, though Islam, Judaism and fringe religions also get a lashing. The film is slick and engaging, apparently presenting well-researched facts that count against religious faith.

One claim is that the story about Jesus is simply one example among many of the dying-rising redeemer god of the ancient world. The god takes many forms – Horus, Mithra, Dionysus – but the story follows a common form. At one point the film reels off a long list of claims about the Egyptian sky god Horus that parallel the life of Jesus. In on-screen text, the film declares that Horus was born of a virgin, baptised by a man later beheaded, worked miracles, walked on water, raised a man called Lazarus from the dead, had twelve disciples, was crucified and after three days rose again from the dead. It all seems rather unsettling and gives the impression that the Gospel accounts are made-up stories reflecting a myth in common currency across the ancient Near East.

But what are the facts? Not a single claim made about Horus in the movie was ever made in the ancient world. It is pure fiction. No one ever claimed Horus was born of a virgin, had twelve disciples or was crucified. Even more significantly, there is no resurrection account of Horus. Bill Maher's claim that these facts are found in the 3,000-year-old Egyptian *Book of the Dead* is entirely fictitious. Yet these bogus claims are promoted by a lavishly made film and witty script. If they are not true, then where did they come from? What seems to be the source are books written by a Victorian poet, Gerald Massey (1828-1907), called *Natural Genesis* and *Ancient Egypt, the Light of the World*. The works have no scholarly weight and are the product of a great imagination. But in popular thought they have been continually recycled, most recently by Tom Harpur in *The Pagan Christ* and the internet documentary *Zeitgeist*.

Adolf Hitler purportedly advised his propagandists with these words: 'Make the lie big, make it simple, keep saying it, and eventually they will believe it.' *Religulous* boldly repeats simple claims that are manifestly untrue. Said enough times, people will think: 'I know that's true … I heard it somewhere…' For Christian apologetics, New Atheism does not require a New Argument because it brings nothing new to the table. What it does demand is that Christians patiently continue to teach the rock-solid credentials for the biblical text and the gospel account of Jesus. It may not appear quite as glitzy or shocking as a Hollywood movie, but it will have the advantage of being true.

FOUR

Christian Marriage is a new idea!

A good football team needs players that can play defensively and those who can play offensively. Evangelism also needs both the defence of truth and a solid offence against the alternatives. While we don't want to be 'offensive', we do need to present a reasoned objection to what else is on offer! During the gay marriage debate, many Christians have been drawn into defensive positions. We want to defend biblical morality, traditional values and marriage. However, we need to remember that apologetics is not only defence, it also means taking on the alternatives.

Many of us have written letters to MPs regarding the gay marriage legislation. That makes for a very interesting exchange of ideas. One of the members of our church received a reply from her MP who was in favour of the legislation. He claimed that the ban on gay marriage was not universal. On the contrary, gay relationships were common in the ancient world. He pointed out, 'It was not outlawed until the Theodosian legal code of A.D. 342 prohibited it.' He was implying that our marriage norm, the quaint and unusual practice of Judaeo-Christianity, was only imposed when Christianity gained influence and nasty old Emperor Theodosius abolished the alternatives. Such a suggestion presents a great opportunity to pose some counter-questions.

What else was outlawed under the reign of Emperor Constantine and the nominally Christian emperors who followed him? Infanticide, the abandoning of newborn babies to die alone and unwanted, was a common form of abortion at birth practised in the classical world. It was outlawed in the newly Christianised Roman Empire. It was also during this time that crucifixion was banned along with the persecution of Christians. Does the fact that a practice was widespread in the ancient world mean it should be a morally acceptable for us? And if the practices of classical Greece and Rome become our standards for today then what other moral reformations are in peril? Do we need to reconsider the age of consent (it was acceptable for adults to have sex with children in the classical world) and what about incest (quite normal among ancient rulers, in fact the preferred option among many royalty)?

The heart of the question we should pose is whether we believe that there are objective moral standards. If there are none, then there is no such thing as moral progress. Like a shifting coastline, moral norms will be reshaped by the tides of fashion. As C.S. Lewis put in his classic, *Mere Christianity*; 'Progress means getting nearer to the place you want to be. And if you have taken a wrong turning, then to go forward does not get you any nearer … the man who turns back soonest is the most progressive man.' What does our society aspire to? What is our moral standard? How do we define the meaning of the golden rule? In Christ there is an answer; outside of Him that question needs to be asked. Many of our politicians are adrift without such an objective moral compass.

FIVE

Religion is in decline

Opinion polls make very interesting, if unreliable, reading. This is demonstrated in the WIN-Gallup 'Religion and Atheism' survey. Based on responses from 51,927 participants in fifty-seven countries during 2012, it seems to indicate a decline in religion since 2005. The global average indicates a rise of 3 per cent in those claiming to be atheists and a decline of 9 per cent in those describing themselves as religious. Stand-out figures include the results from Ireland, which indicate a 22 per cent drop in those claiming to be religious since 2005, coming second to Vietnam which experienced a 23 per cent drop. Of interest to Western evangelicalism is the drop of 13 per cent in those claiming to be religious in the United States, from 73 per cent to 60 per cent. How will that translate into America's cultural exports of films, books, sitcoms and pop music? More detailed figures from the U.K. 2011 census fit the pattern and indicate that 25 per cent of our country do not consider themselves religious.

So how do we interpret this information? One claim might be that atheism is winning the culture wars, and Christianity is fading away. But statistics can be misleading. After all, Richard Dawkins presumably would not claim credit for the decline of religiosity in Vietnam. In fact, while Vietnam showed the greatest decline in those considering themselves religious, it also showed a zero per cent rise in those claiming to be atheist. What does a survey participant mean when they say that they do not consider themselves religious? I am a Christian. I teach theology. I pastor a church. Am I religious? It's not a term I like to use!

The decline in numbers of those considering themselves religious is not directly translated into an increase in atheism or in the popularity of some of the New Atheist diatribes about Christianity. The fact is that the decline in religiosity may be a good thing. It may represent a questioning of nominal faith and traditionalism which, in the long run, could sharpen real, biblical Christianity. The figures from Ireland are instructive here. The dramatic decline in religiosity in Ireland is probably directly related to the child abuse scandals that have rocked her institutional church. Who needs Richard Dawkins when we have churches that behave like this?

Theo Hobson, writing in *The Spectator* (April 2013) under the title 'After the new atheism', comments, 'Richard Dawkins is now seen by many, even many non-believers, as a joke figure, shaking his fist at sky fairies.' As the dust settles, it is far from clear that the new atheists ever generated more light than they did heat. Hobson comments, 'Atheism is still with us. But the movement that threatened to form has petered out.' The decline in religion has not been matched by a rise in atheism.

There is an interesting anomaly in the American figures. In a Gallup poll last month, it was revealed that 77 per cent of Americans believe that religion has lost influence in culture. But the figures also showed that a staggering 75 per cent of Americans believe that this decline is a bad thing and believe that America would be better off if more people were religious. These figures show that, while people are rapidly losing personal confidence in churches, they remain positive about Christianity as a force for good. Our culture stands at a crossroads. The polls show that institutional religion is not in favour. Being counted religious seems old fashioned or antiquated. But atheism has not taken the helm. The decline of religiosity is a decline in formal religious influence. Now is the time not to offer our nation religion – it is tired of that. But this is the time to offer true, personal, living faith grounded in the real historical reliability of the Bible. Now why is it that whenever these polls are conducted no one ever asks me my opinion?

SIX

Christmas is cancelled

Here is the ultimate way to take Christ out of Christmas: deny that He ever existed. That is the claim that has been made from time to time and resurfaced in late 2013 with the fresh promotion of an old book called *Caesar's Messiah: the Roman Conspiracy to Invent Jesus*, along with an accompanying lecture at Conway Hall in London. The *Daily Mail* described the author, Joseph Atwill, as an 'American Bible scholar' who had made the discovery of the non-existence of Jesus through his study of Josephus, the first-century Jewish historian. The *Daily Mail* reported that Atwill, 'does not believe that this is the end of Christianity, but hopes his work will give half-believers a reason to "make a clean break".' Richard Dawkins was quick to circulate a link to Atwill's press release to his 777,000 Twitter followers.

Before we cancel Christmas, let's ask a few questions. Who is Bible scholar Joseph Atwill? What is the substance of his claim? And what does this tell us about our defence of the faith?

Firstly, Joseph Atwill is no Bible scholar. Having made his money in an internet business, he has been able to devote his personal time to reading Josephus. It is not clear that he has read Josephus in Greek and he makes no claim to any relevant professional training. Nor has he subjected any of his claims to peer review and has little support from the academic community. He is no more a Bible scholar than anyone else who has read some of the Bible. This may help explain his outlandish proposal.

Atwill argues that a Roman imperial family invented the Jesus story as a way of pacifying the Jewish people. A single author created the hoax much later in the first century in order to subvert Judaism and make the people more amenable to Roman rule. Atwill discovered this supposed truth by reading Josephus's *The Jewish War* in which the secret was supposed to be encoded. Therefore, not only Jesus, but Christianity itself did not exist before A.D. 70. So, is it time to pack away the Christmas decorations and cancel the turkey?

There is no substance to Atwill's claim. The evidence for the existence of Christianity is already abundant prior to A.D. 70. Roman historians refer to the existence of the movement. The New Testament does not only include a number of independent gospel accounts of Jesus but the writings of the apostles, including Paul, which secular scholars agree date to the A.D. 50s. Scholars argue over the identity of Jesus, but there is no serious doubt of His historical existence. Even the sceptical professor Bart Ehrman dismisses this conspiracy theory nonsense. Atwill's own reconstruction is a superficial reading of Josephus and a ludicrous interpretation of how the Roman Empire dealt with its subject nations.

Atheist scientist and vocal critic of Christianity, P.Z. Myers, describes Atwill's proposal as 'ridiculous' on his blog. He poses the interesting question, 'How can smart atheists be bamboozled by Joseph Atwill?' (Dawkins among them). There are probably many reasons, not least an intellectual bias against Christ. Joseph Atwill's work is a wonderful example of clutching at straws! However, I wonder, could Christmas be part of the problem?

Our somewhat fanciful and embellished retellings of the Nativity during the season are not thick with historical facts. And as for the fun, but far-fetched, traditions that we add on to our celebrations, could they not blur the lines between truth and fairy tale? I love this time of year, and there are traditions worth cherishing, but let us make sure that nothing confuses the solid, historical truth-telling at the heart of our worship.

Part 2

Talk about History

SEVEN

Christian Urban Legends

When I am teaching Old Testament, a student will sometimes ask me if I have heard that Pharaoh's chariot wheels from the Exodus have been located in the depths of the Red Sea. It is exciting stuff, and often based on grainy photographs passed about on the Internet and on Christian DVDs. Sadly, it is a hoax, which has undermined the credibility of evangelical engagement with archaeology and other disciplines.

The problems with the evidence are manifold. We ought to be unsettled by the fact that no academic, objective scrutiny of the claims has ever been made. The central evidence itself is based on the personal testimony of the late Ron Wyatt, who took some photographs of what looks like coral-encrusted ship debris and made lavish claims for its significance without any rigorous testing. On investigation, every element of his evidence looks decidedly shaky! Perhaps we should not be too harsh on Wyatt. He was a busy man. Travelling on holidays, he also claimed to have discovered Noah's Ark (a different one to the ark found by the team in our first essay!), the Ark of the Covenant, and a number of other important biblical relics. I have no hesitation in turning students away from this kind of sensational but unsubstantiated hokum.

However, underlying these claims is a more important issue. Our evangelical churches can become an undiscerning haven for fraudulent ideas and untested rumours. Such threadbare evidence is woven into sermons and youth talks. Unlikely proofs become a church equivalent of an urban legend, sounding more plausible for frequent retelling. Does it matter? Yes, because we undermine our credibility and our integrity. If friends discover that we have slipped one hoax into our evangelism, then how will they know they can trust any other piece of historical or archaeological information? If photographs of chariot wheels are demonstrably spurious, then does that undermine the Exodus itself? What about the reliability of the Old Testament? Can we trust the Bible at all?

We must double-check our facts in evangelism. A Google search is not enough! There should be a healthy distrust of the first thing we read and a careful weighing up of what evidence we use with our friends. Eternal matters are at stake. The Bible describes events that really happened, and we can be confident in our faith. But we do not need the hogwash. There is a wealth of solid scholarship that supports the essential historical credentials of the Bible. It is this kind of scholarship that we should be circulating in our evangelical circles. Let's guard against the baloney.

EIGHT

Just how many Gospels are there?

Which is your favourite Gospel? Matthew? John? What about the Gospel of Thomas? Or Barnabas? Or Philip? Or Mary, Nicodemus or Judas? 'Gospels' bearing these names can be found in the ancient world. So, have we got a censored version of the life of Jesus in our New Testament? Do we need to read these additional gospels in case there is something we haven't been told?

Dan Brown played on these concerns to great effect in his best-selling *Da Vinci Code* novel. One of his characters, the historian Sir Leigh Teabing, claims: 'Some of the gospels that Constantine attempted to eradicate managed to survive. The Dead Sea Scrolls were found in the 1950s hidden in a cave near Qumran in the Judean desert. And, of course, the Coptic Scrolls in 1945 at Nag Hammadi...' With claims like these, the general impression given is that our New Testament is a selective compilation, ignoring a vast array of rival accounts of Jesus. This impression comes from a misunderstanding of the dating of the gospels.

It is true that there are many gospels from the time of the early church. But not all were written anywhere near the time of Jesus.

The Gospel of Barnabas is popular among Muslims and presents an account of Jesus entirely at odds with the New Testament. The earliest manuscript copy is sixteenth century and the original edition was no earlier than the late Middle Ages. Written in Spanish and in Italian, it betrays its late

Mediterranean origins with a description of wine stored in wooden casks – not something used at the time of Jesus.

The Gospel of Judas made a stir in 2006 when the National Geographic Society published a translation of a copy dating to about A.D. 300. It presents a more favourable account of the life of Judas Iscariot. Despite the popular stir, the scholars behind the translation did not argue that it contained any historical insights into the life of Jesus – it is a much later work of a heretical movement called Gnosticism.

The Gnostic movement is the source of many of these rival gospels. Developing later in the second century, it fused Greek philosophical ideas with Christianity. Gnosis means 'knowledge' and the emphasis in this movement was on a secret knowledge unknown to the masses. They produced a number of gospels which are quite alien to the first-century Hebrew world of Jesus. Gnostic gospels include the Gospel of Peter and the Gospel of Philip. No serious scholar suggests that any of these gospels were written by the first-century characters after whom they are named. In fact, many of these gospels are part of what is now known as the Nag Hammadi collection.

Nag Hammadi is a location on the River Nile north of Luxor. In 1945, several books were found hidden in the desert sands. Preserved in the dry Egyptian climate, the books were over 1,500 years old. Interestingly, no New Testament gospels were found among the collection but only the later Gnostic texts. Immediately this suggested that their burial was a deliberate attempt to hide books that had been declared fraudulent during that time. Otherwise, why would no canonical gospel be found among them?

Their tone and content are quite different from the world of the New Testament. The four biblical Gospels are rooted in history, full of geographical observations, laden with Aramaic phrases and Hebrew idioms. They breathe their authenticity and are universally accepted to be first-century texts. They were in wide circulation by the second century and even without direct copies we are able to piece together their existence from countless citations in secondary literature, letters and sermons from the time. If you meet anyone intrigued by the alternative Gnostic gospels, then why not suggest they try reading them? The translations by James Robinson are easily available and accurate. Most people will quickly give up reading them, but those who persevere will recognise the quite different quality to that of the biblical Gospels.

Rolex watches are considered desirable and so markets around the world are flooded with fake Rolexes. The existence of fake gospels should not surprise us either. The Nag Hammadi collection helps our case – their grand, philosophical style highlights the simple, historical authenticity of Matthew, Mark, Luke and John. And what of Sir Leigh Teabing's reference to 'The Dead Sea Scrolls' of Qumran? Not a single scrap of a Gnostic gospel was found among them. Yet again, the case against the New Testament is built more on rumour and insinuation than on a careful consideration of the facts.

NINE

Darwin's Deathbed Conversion

Have you heard the story of Charles Darwin's deathbed conversion? In his final months, he was visited at home by a Lady Hope, who later described the encounter. One summer afternoon at his home, restricted to his bedroom by ill health, he declared his faith in Jesus and confessed of his theory: 'I was a young man with unformed ideas. I threw out queries, suggestions ... People made a religion of them.' Therefore, preachers will tell us, we should share Darwin's mature opinion of his unformed ideas, reject evolution and embrace Christ.

It's a great story, if only it were true. It has become one of many Christian 'urban legends' that do the rounds in popular sermons and books. It has been retold so many times that it has passed into Christian folklore. It reminds me of the often-told explanation of the 'eye of the needle'. We are assured that Jesus never intended this to refer to a literal needle, but rather to a smaller entrance in a larger city gate allowing the passage of unburdened camels late at night. These stories are not true, but are so appealing and told so often that they almost sound like Scripture!

So what of Darwin's deathbed conversion? Disentangling the facts from the fiction is almost impossible. Its origins are traced to a 1915 letter written by Lady Hope to a newspaper. Her recollections need not imply anything like a religious conversion on Darwin's part. As far as we know, Darwin remained agnostic to the end. But what truth is there in the story? James Moore, a highly respected biographer of Darwin, has researched the anecdote in great detail and his conclusions are probably as much as we will ever know. The Lady Hope of the letter was an itinerant social worker and evangelist who probably did visit Darwin at his home during the last months of his life, while she was involved in outreach work in his village. Her recollections are ambiguous at best and possibly exaggerated, but there was a genuine engagement between Darwin and these itinerant evangelists.

During the harvest, labourers would arrive from around the country looking for seasonal work. They found employment in the harvest and they were paid, but generally the money was then lost in drinking, leaving families in poverty at home. Darwin was concerned about this and engaged in humanitarian efforts to help these men. The efforts were a failure. But Darwin was impressed with the work of the evangelists. Writing to a 'tent preacher', who had asked for financial assistance, he commented: 'We have never been able to reclaim a drunkard, but through your services I do not know that there is one drunkard left in the village' (James Moore, *The Darwin Legend*, p. 47).

Now here is an anecdote of real apologetic value. We are all concerned for the plight of the vulnerable and bringing purpose to life. Can Darwinian humanitarianism or secular humanism do it? Consider the power of the gospel to change lives and transform societies. Even the most obstinate atheist cannot ignore it. A gentler agnostic like Darwin could see it clearly.

Christianity is true, and Christianity works. That is a powerful combination to appeal to all people. We present our case for Christianity best with coherent evidence and honest anecdotes. It is hard for a rich man to enter the kingdom of God. In fact, it is like getting a camel through the eye of a needle. That isn't just really hard, like squeezing through a small city gate, that's impossible. But, Jesus said, with God all things are possible. The power of a truthful message and a loving witness may be all we need to demolish strongholds of unbelief. There is no need for embellishment; the truth can look after itself!

TEN

A Footprint in Solomon's Temple

Was there a real King Solomon or is he a legendary figure of Israelite imagination? As evidence of his existence we should be able to point to monumental architecture. One possible example is the six-chambered city gates associated with his reign, some of which have been revealed by archaeology (1 Kings 9:15). But is there any material evidence for the temple from the time of Solomon? Some would say no. They would use this lack of visible evidence to undermine what the Bible claims for Israel's golden age under his united monarchy. However, there is important evidence for the first temple that has been visible, though ignored, all along!

Direct evidence for the temple of Solomon is difficult to find. The area of the temple mount has been extensively redeveloped over the centuries. The temple built by Solomon was destroyed by the Babylonians in 586 B.C. When the Jews later returned to resettle Jerusalem, they built a more modest temple in the same location. By the time of Jesus, King Herod had practically rebuilt this second temple and greatly expanded the platform on which it was situated. After the Romans destroyed this Herodian temple in A.D. 70, there followed a pagan temple, early church structure and an Islamic shrine. The site of the temple is today dominated by the Islamic shrine called the Dome of the Rock. With its beautiful blue and white tiles and famous golden dome, this forms Jerusalem's most iconic image. It also poses a major obstacle to any attempt to recover evidence for the much earlier temple of Solomon. On the most sensitive piece of real estate in the world, archaeological excavation is nearly impossible.

The Dome of the Rock covers the natural rocky outcrop which was probably once the peak of Mount Moriah, where Abraham took his son Isaac. The only reason why this natural area of rock should have remained exposed in Herod's great rebuilding work is that it was itself part of the original Holy of Holies. In a curious irony, the great Islamic structure which has stood for longer than any of the Israelite temples has probably served to protect the most venerated spot in Judaism.

So what direct evidence is left of Solomon's temple? The authenticity of a small, carved pomegranate which may have once formed the tip of a priest's sceptre has been subject to some dispute. Many have considered it the only direct, material link to the first temple. However, Dutch archaeological architect Leen Ritmeyer has identified more startling evidence for Solomon's temple.

The Holy of Holies housed the Ark of the Covenant. While the ark has long since been lost, Ritmeyer has identified a footprint of its existence. In 1994 he was examining photographs of the rock. Once the dimensions of the first temple are overlaid with the present temple mount, a section of the exposed outcrop aligns with the original Holy of Holies. Dead centre in this sacred space, Ritmeyer noticed a rectangular depression carved in the rock. In biblical terms it measured 1.5 by 2.5 cubits. That is the size of the ark. The uneven rock surface had a level space at its centre for the ark to stand upon. While the ark probably disappeared with the destruction of the first temple, its presence has left a mark. The evidence has been there all along, surviving the refurbishments of Romans, Muslims, Crusaders and modern renovation. You can read about this important discovery in Leen Ritmeyer's *The Quest*, published by Carta in 2006.

Christians believe in the existence of the first temple because they trust the Bible as a reliable record of history. Sceptics will scorn this faith because they will point to areas where historical evidence is lacking. But whenever material evidence of the past emerges it confirms the reliability of the biblical account. Nothing has yet emerged to contradict the claims we read in the Bible. British scholar Kenneth Kitchen has pointed out that 'the absence of evidence is not the same as evidence of absence.' If there is something in the Bible for which we do not have evidence, perhaps we ought to say that we do not yet have evidence. Maybe, like Solomon's temple, the evidence is there, we just have not seen it .... yet!

ELEVEN

The Discovery of Sodom

The name of the city of Sodom has become a byword for sin and the city itself has passed into the world of legend and mythology. But did this city really exist and is the story of its destruction at the hand of God a real, historical event? Questions like these matter to our defence of the reliability of the earliest passages of Scripture.

Theories about the lost cities of Sodom and Gomorrah have included claims that they lie beneath the waters of the Dead Sea or are identified with ruins at the southern end of the Dead Sea. But none of these suggestions have led to any solid evidence in their favour. So where is the evidence for this ancient cataclysm and the destruction of these cities?

Archaeologist Steven Collins has now published his claim to have found Sodom (Steven Collins and Latayne C. Scott, *Discovering the City of Sodom*, New York: Howard Books, 2013) and submitted his evidence to a recent issue of *The Biblical Archaeology Review* ('Where is Sodom? The Case for Tall el-Hammam' March/April 2013). Tall (or Tel) el-Hammam in Jordan is a site north of the Dead Sea where his team have been excavating for eight years. Why is he persuaded that this can be identified as Sodom?

The remarkable fact about Collins's claim is that it arises from the guidance of the text of the Bible. According to Genesis, Sodom was visible from Bethel and Ai and located in what is called the 'plain' of the Jordan (Gen. 13:10). When Sodom was destroyed, the smoke of its destruction could also be seen by Abraham from this vantage point (Gen. 19:28). These geographical clues rule out the southern end of the Dead Sea as a possible location for Sodom. Only the northern end would be visible from this central hill country. But there is a further geographical clue. The Hebrew word translated 'plain' really means a round disc. From Bethel a fertile circle of land is visible spanning both sides of the River Jordan. On the western edge of this disc is the city of Jericho. On the eastern edge lies Tall el-Hammam. These were the geographical clues that pointed Collins towards this particular Bronze Age ruin.

Of course, no 'Welcome to Sodom' sign has been dug up by archaeologists. However, what has been found reveals an impressive city dating to the time of Abraham. The enormous fortified walls include sections that are 100ft thick. The imposing gateway fits the description of the location where the angels met Lot (Gen. 19:1). There is plentiful archaeological evidence for the sudden destruction of Sodom. A thick layer of ash and charred walls all bear witness to destruction by fire. After this destruction the site was unoccupied for hundreds of years, and other sites in the region were also abandoned. What caused this destruction?

A further intriguing find has been investigated by Collins and his team. Across the site melted pottery has been found, with one side still intact and the other side turned to a greenish glaze through intense heat. To produce this kind of damage there needed to be a sudden high temperature followed by quick cooling. What could cause this kind of scorching? Similar greenish desert glass is found elsewhere in the world and its origins are not geological. In fact, Collins was able to draw upon two similar forms of glass. One form is found in the deserts of Egypt and results from a meteor impact. It was considered a precious stone and was even found as jewellery in the tomb of Tutankhamen. The other example is found in the deserts of New Mexico. They formed during the atom bomb tests when the superheated blast wave melted the sand. We do not know exactly how God destroyed Sodom and Gomorrah. That the traces of destruction should resemble what would be left in the wake of a thermonuclear explosion would fit with the description that 'the LORD rained down burning sulphur ... out of the heavens ... destroying all those living in the cities, and also the vegetation in the land ... dense smoke rising from the land, like the smoke from a furnace' (Gen. 19:24-28).

So can we say that Sodom has been found? There remains a problem. The destruction level dates to 1650 B.C., about 150 years after the traditional dating of Abraham's lifetime. But our understanding of the biblical dates may be wrong and the dating of the site may yet be adjusted. Collins has certainly made a good case for his claim. For Christians, these are more scientific reasons to read the Bible as a reliable witness to history. More than that, we have another reminder to take seriously the warnings of Scripture. Judgment days of the past are not the stuff of myth and legend but real historical events. Likewise, the judgment day of the future will be a real event involving cosmic forces; 'But the day of the Lord will come like a thief. The heavens will disappear with a roar; the elements will be destroyed by fire, and the earth and everything done in it will be laid bare' (2 Pet. 3:10). We have been warned.

TWELVE

Defending the book of Daniel

Some Bible books have a harder time than others being accepted as historically reliable. Among the Old Testament books, Daniel often takes a beating. The critical reaction frequently reflects a sceptical attitude to miracles (did Daniel really spend a night in a den of lions?) or to predictive prophecy (was Daniel really able to predict the rise and fall of later empires?). As a consequence, many critics date these books late and suggest they are Jewish legends with prophecies of events that had already taken place included to make them sound authentic.

We may be tempted to sidestep these criticisms by suggesting they don't really matter or that they have little bearing on our preaching of the gospel. But that evasion is short-sighted. If we reject something as spurious because it contains miracles or accurate predictive prophecy, then eventually that attitude will undermine the gospel. What is left of the ministry of Jesus if we reject miracles? What is left of the gospel if we reject prophecy of future events?

It is ironic that all the accumulating archaeological and material evidence supports the reliability of Daniel, while nothing has been found to undermine it. S.R. Driver (1846-1914), professor of Hebrew at Oxford University, wrote one of the most influential commentaries on Daniel and dated its final form to what is called the Maccabean period (c.165 B.C.). This was long after the Babylonian exile (c.609-536 B.C.) in which the book claims to be set.

One reason Driver gave is the book's use of Aramaic, rather than Hebrew, which we know would come into fashion closer to the time of the New Testament. However, another reason must surely be the presence of predictive prophecy. Daniel predicts a succession of kingdoms following the Babylonians. If he wrote these around 580 B.C., then his vision of the future proved remarkably accurate. If they were written in 165 B.C., then there is no miraculous element, just a good memory of the past!

As a matter of fact, Driver's redating of Daniel still fails to deny its predictive content. Daniel predicts four empires of which the fourth is clearly a description of Rome. Even placing Daniel in the time of the Maccabees still puts it a century prior to the rise of Rome in the region. To get around this, critics had to include an extra empire between Persia and Greece. The bizarre result is that they denied Daniel the ability to accurately predict the future but attributed to him a very clumsy recording of the past.

However, what do we know since Driver published his commentary that might help us date the Book of Daniel? Quite a lot – and nothing that would support Driver's theory.

Most importantly, the discovery of the Dead Sea Scrolls from 1947 onwards has provided a vast number of ancient biblical texts that enable us to have much greater confidence in the reliability of the copying of the Bible. The Dead Sea Scrolls include eight copies of Daniel, along with several related writings that use material from the book. Prior to the discovery of the Dead Sea Scrolls, the earliest complete text of Daniel in Hebrew dated to the tenth century A.D. The earliest Dead Sea texts of Daniel are dated to 125 B.C.. As these are copies of copies, they point to a much earlier date for the original.

Furthermore, the Dead Sea scrolls have shown that the presence of Aramaic in the book does not point to a late date but actually forms evidence for an early date.

Aramaic scripts and vocabulary of the Dead Sea copies demonstrate a much earlier form than those of other second-century B.C. examples. In other words, far from indicating a late date, the Aramaic used in Daniel now suggests a much earlier date than critics like Driver could have known. In fact, scholars now suggest that the Aramaic used in Daniel is of a form originating in Babylon rather than Judea. The origins of the book lie in a period much earlier than Driver guessed and a location far from Jerusalem. The form of Aramaic is pre-500 B.C., and the location is Babylonian not Palestinian.

The evidence of the Dead Sea Scrolls bolsters our continuing confidence in Daniel and consigns more recent commentaries to the dustbins of history! Of course, this brief essay only scratches the surface of the value of the Dead Sea Scrolls for apologetics. For much more detail, I would recommend Randall Price, *Secrets of the Dead Sea Scrolls* (Harvest House, 1996) or, for a more up-to-date survey, John J. Collins and Craig A. Evans (eds.), *Christian Beginnings and the Dead Sea Scrolls* (Baker Books, 2006). It is also worth noting that there is a wealth of nonsense written on the Dead Sea Scrolls. Much of this was a result of the air of conspiracy that surrounded the slow publication of scroll translations. Since all the manuscripts are now publically accessible in translation, books making outlandish claims about the Dead Sea Scrolls are gradually disappearing. However, the desert region around the Dead Sea remains a favourable location to preserve ancient manuscripts and so there is a good chance that more will be discovered in the years to come!

THIRTEEN

The Disappearing Towns of Jesus

Bethlehem. Nazareth. These are the places most associated with the life of Jesus before He began His public ministry. Therefore, what better way to dismiss the Christian faith than claim that these towns never existed at the time of Jesus? They are the product of later, fanciful legends and promoted as a way of making a fast shekel out of religious tourism. James Randi, a popular American magician and an atheist, boldly declares, 'There simply is no demonstrable evidence from the Nazareth site that dates to the time of Jesus Christ.'

A similar claim is made regarding Bethlehem. Though it was occupied in earlier times, some say it was abandoned during the time of Jesus. Israeli archaeologist Aviram Oshri has identified a different Bethlehem, nearer Nazareth, as thriving at the time of Jesus. Oshri comments, 'It makes much more sense that Mary rode on a donkey, while she was at the end of the pregnancy, from Nazareth to Bethlehem of Galilee, which is only seven kilometres, than the other Bethlehem, which is 150 kilometres' (*NPR News*). The fact that the Gospels nowhere mention a donkey does not instil confidence in Oshri's research. But what about the facts? Were Bethlehem and Nazareth inhabited during the early years of Jesus?

Bethlehem is sometimes dismissed because the Church of the Nativity that tourists visit only dates from A.D. 327, long after the time of Jesus. But the question to ask is why was a church to venerate the Nativity built here? The history of association with the Nativity is much older. Justin Martyr

(c. A.D. 100-165), who lived only forty miles from Bethlehem, identified a cave in the town as the site of Christ's birth. Origen (c. A.D. 185-254) describes visiting the cave himself. Over two hundred years of tradition, before the church was built, identify the site and give it authenticity. Furthermore, Bethlehem has revealed evidence of first-century occupation, including pottery from that time.

What about Nazareth? In some ways, the first-century evidence is quite similar to that of Bethlehem. There is no evidence of a large city, monumental buildings or wealthy citizens at the time of Jesus. But there is evidence for an agricultural community. Pottery, a winepress and burial caves have borne witness to this period of habitation. In 2009, archaeologists revealed the remains of a stone-built house dating to the time of Jesus. It is estimated that Nazareth was a hamlet of about fifty houses during the first century.

First-century Nazareth and Bethlehem were the kind of locations that leave little evidence in the archaeological record. Little wealth means no monumental buildings and few coins or durable goods. However, new material continues to come to light. A discovery of an ancient bathhouse in 1993 may yet prove that Nazareth was more significant at the time of Jesus than previously thought.

Critics dismiss the Gospels because there is no evidence for the 'cities' of Nazareth or Bethlehem at the time of Jesus. This objection arises from a misunderstanding of the Greek word 'polis' often translated 'town' or even 'city' (Matt. 2:23; Luke 2:4). But what is the difference between a hamlet, village, town or city? A textbook on town planning would need a precision over words like village or town that need not apply elsewhere. Matthew and Luke are not using this term in some technical sense. Their concerns are not with town planning but with recording history.

There is no reason to doubt the existence of Bethlehem and Nazareth but there is reason to think again if we imagine them as large, wealthy cities. The reason to think again is because of what the Bible itself says. Of Nazareth, Nathanael asked, 'Can anything good come from there?' (John 1:46). Of Bethlehem, prophecy already indicated its obscurity at the time of Christ's birth. As the New Living Translation puts it, 'But you, O Bethlehem Ephrathah, are only a small village among all the people of Judah' (Micah 5:2). Jesus did not hail from a great city like London, New York or even Jerusalem but from obscurity. Which leaves us the question, why do we still know so much more about this one man than His home towns? We don't worship sacred sites but we do worship a historical Saviour.

Part 3

Talk about the Big Questions

FOURTEEN

What about all the world religions?

A king invites ten blindfolded men into his courtyard where an elephant stands. Each one feels a part of the animal's bulk and describes what they have found.

One grasps the tail and thinks it's a snake. Another strokes the hide and describes a wall. Still another touches a tusk and believes it is a spear. Poor elephant! The story is a parable originating from Buddhist traditions. It is used to provide an analogy for the world religions. Religious people describe God as Allah, or Brahman or Christ, but that just reflects their limited point of view. Like the misunderstood elephant in the parable, the God behind the world religions is misdescribed by his sincere devotees.

Theologian John Hick (1922-2012) built his reputation on promoting the radical claim that all the major world religions are responding to the same God. The parable of the blind men and the elephant is a good description of Hick's claim. Hick has provided a detailed, philosophical case for what is sometimes called 'pluralism', but this simple image is widely popular today. Isn't it arrogant to claim that there is only one path to God? Surely we are most likely to believe in the religion of our parents or our society? Doesn't that suggest it is narrow-minded to believe that there is an exclusive way of salvation?

Hick maintained this view for over thirty years of his scholarly career and published many works to defend or extend it. One problem emerges very clearly with religious pluralism. If all religions are responding to the same divine being, then what is this being really like? One obvious point is that we can't call it 'God'. Some religions believe in a god, but others are atheistic (Zen Buddhism) or regard god as irrelevant (Confucianism). So what does Hick do? He replaces God with the 'Ultimate Real'. What is this Ultimate Real? To be compatible with all religions, it must be beyond any of our descriptions. Hick states that the Ultimate Real must be beyond good or evil, beyond existing or not existing, beyond being personal or non-personal. The trouble is, with an Ultimate Reality so beyond all definition, it is little different from an Ultimate Nothing.

Pluralists affirm that all religions are equally valid. There are many paths to God. It all sounds so tolerant. But don't believe a word of it! Pluralism is as much a claim that all religions are equally false as equally true. What is missing in the popular retelling of the parable of the blind men and the elephant? The king is the one who can see the elephant and point out the limitations of those who are blindfolded. The king has the best seat in the house. While Hick may dismiss evangelicals as arrogant, we mustn't lose sight of the fact that the pluralist is also sneaking into the chair of the king. They are occupying a commanding position from which to judge all religions as equally wrong and equally right. But the flimsy foundations of this vantage point are philosophical speculation and politically correct analogies.

As Christians, we believe in a King who has revealed Himself. He has spoken and revealed that a personal God exists, is good and has provided the only way of salvation through Christ. Given a choice between the speculation of pluralism or the revelation of Scripture, I know which path I choose! Not all roads lead to Rome and many paths lead far away from God. Speculation may suggest that many doors are open. Revelation points to one door. Jesus said, 'I am the way and the truth and the life. No one comes to the Father except through me' (John 14:6). Ultimately it is not a question of which religion do we trust but who do we listen to? Great religious founders or prophets like the Buddha, or Isaiah or Mohammed claim to be signposts. Jesus Christ uniquely claims to be the road itself. He does not point us somewhere else; He draws us to Himself.

FIFTEEN

Who was Jesus?

For all the various arguments and debates for and against Christianity, eventually we must focus on Christ. Who was Jesus?

This is the question to which all our conversations should lead. Apologetics is a pointless pursuit if its ultimate end is not the presentation of the gospel of Jesus.

Generally, Jesus has been revered and admired, if not worshipped, by all those who have read the Gospels. Mahatma Gandhi, the Hindu religious reformer, asked: 'What, then, does Jesus mean to me? To me, He was one of the greatest teachers humanity has ever had' (Gandhi, *What Jesus Means to Me*, R.K. Prabhu).

Albert Einstein, the agnostic Jewish scientist, was asked about his view of Jesus in a newspaper interview. His reply was striking: 'No one can read the Gospels without feeling the actual presence of Jesus. His personality pulsates in every word. No myth is filled with such life. How different, for instance, is the impression which we receive from an account of legendary heroes of antiquity like Theseus. Theseus and other heroes of his type lack the authentic vitality of Jesus' (Albert Einstein, *Saturday Evening Post* interview, 1929).

Vincent Van Gogh, the post-Impressionist artist, found inspiration in the Jesus of the Gospels: 'He lived serenely, as a greater artist than all other artists, despising marble and clay as well as colour, working in living flesh' (Van Gogh, 'Letter to Emile Bernard'). Jews, Hindus, Buddhists and Muslims have found something to admire in Jesus. Artists, military commanders, composers and industrial leaders have found inspiration in Jesus.

But what does someone, who would admire Jesus without worshipping Him as Lord and Saviour, do with His exclusive claims? How can someone admire Jesus as a good teacher when His teachings reveal His divinity (John 10:33). A common strategy is to pretend there are two people: a Jesus we like and a Jesus we don't like. We can then hold on to what we like (we call him the real Jesus) and ditch the characteristics we don't like (we can call Him the Jesus of church invention). This way of managing Jesus has been popular for the past 200 years. A new version appeared as a best-selling novel by children's author Philip Pullman.

Pullman was challenged by Archbishop Rowan Williams to write a story about the life of Jesus. The result was *The Good Man Jesus and the Scoundrel Christ* (Canongate 2010). The story tells of how a young, unmarried girl had a one-night stand and gave birth to twins. One she called Jesus. He grew up to be a wise and thoughtful man who would one day be crucified, a victim of his own popularity. The other was a sickly child whom she called Christ. He grew up to be a liar and fantasist who manipulated his brother so that an organised religion could be built around him.

On the death of Jesus, the scoundrel Christ, being his twin, was mistaken for a resurrected appearance of his brother and so a legend was born. The names of the brothers became forever fused as the Jesus Christ of Christian theology.

Rather than appealing to historical evidence or research, Pullman writes an imaginative story (preventing a critic from making this obvious point: Philip, you have made all this up!). The main aim of his retelling is to separate an admirable, if misunderstood, Jesus from a nasty, manipulative Christ.

This attempt to divide the Jesus of history from the Christ of faith has been rehashed over the past 200 years by various theologians and thinkers. And it is a failure. Such projects always tell us more about their authors than about their subject. In 1909, the Catholic theologian George Tyrrell made a perceptive comment on the attempt by liberal theologians to discover the historical Jesus. Their reconstructed Jesus was always 'the reflection of a liberal Protestant face, seen at the bottom of a deep well' (George Tyrrell, *Christianity at the Crossroads*). In other words, the Jesus they thought they had brought to light was simply a reflection of what they admired, or wanted to admire, in themselves. Likewise, Philip Pullman's novel tells us a great deal about the author's presuppositions, but next to nothing about the historical Jesus.

But all of these attempts do serve to reinforce the enduring fascination with the penniless preacher from Nazareth. Both the vague, limp, reconstructed Jesus of the Martin Scorsese film adaptation of *The Last Temptation of Christ* and the figment of Pullman's imagination only highlight their obvious weakness. Those reconstructed Christs could never have caused the earthquake of history that would bring down empires, raise up artists and poets, capture the admiration of religious leaders and inspire bold social reformation.

To explain the real impact of Jesus, something more is needed. To find that something more, we need to encourage our friends to turn from works of fiction and read the Gospels for themselves.

It is here that they are confronted by someone who is no mere man. This is not another moral teacher, thoughtful philosopher or political revolutionary. Such people come and go. But not Jesus. The enduring legacy of Jesus is a result of His unchanging identity as the God who became man, who now continues to speak, command and transform through His Word. If there is one positive result from all the attempts to undermine the historical Jesus, it is that some will turn to the Gospels and read for themselves of the One who cannot be pressed into a shape of our own choosing.

SIXTEEN

What do the Heavens declare?

The death of Patrick Moore at the age of 89 on 9 December 2012 brought out a host of warm tributes to one of the most colourful and eccentric television personalities. As the host of *The Sky at Night* for so much of our lifetime, and a regular contributor on television when a space-related issue emerged, he became part of the furniture of contemporary culture. Following Patrick Moore, Brian Cox seems to be taking up the mantle of being the U.K.'s public face of astronomy. The popularity of his documentaries and the BBC *Stargazing Live* shows demonstrate the continuing public interest in the night sky.

God commends astronomy (Gen. 15:5). It is God who gives the stars their names (Isa. 40:26), and we should recognise the beauty of the constellations (Job 38:31-32; Song 6:10). However, there are a number of issues for the defence of our faith that arise with astronomy.

In the ancient world, the great danger of the heavens was found in astrology. In fact, the differences between astrology and astronomy were blurred and to study the stars was also to try to find meaning for our lives in their patterns. Moses deliberately avoids the common words for sun and moon, preferring to call them 'great lights' (Gen. 1:16), in order to avoid associations of divinity. The great lights are not there to be worshipped but to be markers for the seasons. Ancient Israelites and later Christians were often sidetracked into astrology. Moses warned the Israelites not to worship the stars (Deut. 4:19), and 'divination' is regularly condemned (Deut. 18:9-11).

Astrology remains a lure in the contemporary world but those who pursue astronomy are quick to reject it. When Patrick Moore was asked if horoscopes had any merit, he replied; 'The only thing astrology proves is that there is one born every minute.' But in their dismissal of astrology some astronomers sneak in a dismissal of all things supernatural. There is often a subtle but persuasive appeal to a materialistic view of the cosmos. Brian Cox, an amiable atheist (unlike Richard Dawkins, who could be characterised as an aggressive example!), produced an engaging and stylish presentation on what we know about the stars in his *Wonders of the Universe* series. But the episodes do not simply present the facts and theories. Cox also provides a philosophy of human nature. So in the first episode he tells us, 'Life in the universe will only exist for a fleeting, bright instant in time because life is just a temporary structure on the long road from order to disorder ... our true significance lies in our ability and desire to explore this beautiful universe.'

But this is not science. It is philosophy. It is a philosophical view founded on guesswork because even our understanding of the material universe is incomplete. Brian Cox is well aware that our understanding of the material universe is itself limited. In a 2011 interview with Nancy Atkinson, he comments, 'What is 96 per cent of the Universe made of? We know our Universe is full of something called Dark Matter and we don't know what it is. The Universe is accelerating in its expansion, which we call Dark Energy and we don't know what that is either.' This is honest and perceptive. But if we need to be cautious about what exactly makes up 96 per cent of the material universe, then surely a scientist needs to be cautious in offering a philosophy of life on the basis of our limited observations?

The Bible encourages astronomy but challenges our interpretation: 'The heavens declare the glory of God; the skies proclaim the work of his hands. Day after day they pour forth speech; night after night they reveal knowledge.' (Ps. 19:1-2). The stars speak of a universe formed in a moment of creation with the perfect conditions for stability and the existence of intelligent life. The stars point to the existence of an intelligent, loving and powerful Creator. In our witness to friends, we should reclaim the stars from the paganism of astrology and the materialism of atheists. The wonder of the universe is a powerful clue to the existence of God.

SEVENTEEN

Is the Bible an immoral book?

Attempts to visualise the Bible in films or TV series remind us just how much violence the Old Testament records. For the average non-Christian viewer or filmgoer it may reinforce their suspicion that the God of the Old Testament is a God of anger and malevolence, unsuited to our modern morals.

It is important to maintain that God is a judge who has the right to dispense judgment. He is the creator, and we are the creation. His judgments are fair and wise by definition. Whether the flood at the time of Noah or the day of judgment when Christ returns, history displays the justice and sovereignty of God.

But many of the so-called 'terror texts' still need some explanation. Why did God command the Israelites to destroy the Canaanite towns? Do the laws of the Old Testament seem harsh in our modern world?

We do not read the Bible without giving proper attention to context and genre. Many of the most violent passages in Scripture are descriptive rather than prescriptive – they describe what went on rather than prescribe how we should behave. The book of Judges is particularly representative of this. It is hard to find a good moral example in its pages. But the book itself tells us that: 'In those days Israel had no king and everyone did as he saw fit' (Judg. 21:25).

In the book of Joshua, we read of God's judgement on the entire Canaanite population through the Israelites. This can be harder to interpret. It is a divine decree. It reflects God's judgment on a wicked people when their sin had reached 'full measure' (Gen. 15:16). However, we may still be perplexed at the judgment falling upon children and animals.

It helps to pause and read these stories a little more closely. The description of total destruction is normal ancient Near-Eastern warfare language. In practice, Israel did not totally destroy the Canaanites. Many lived on in the land and Jerusalem would remain in the hands of the Jebusites until the time of King David. Also, the destruction brought about by the Israelites fell upon the cities, essentially fortress strongholds. Many people would have lived and worked on the land and fled long before. A city like Jericho would have been more like a castle standing against the Israelites. It was a military target.

But we still question why God brought about destruction of all its inhabitants. The theological answer is that God cared about the purity of His people in their new land. As they settled in the land, they were tempted by the local religious practices, like child sacrifice and prostitution. In order to create a space for any hope of a dedicated people of Israel, God had to destroy what was there. This is not ethnic cleansing. Some of these ethnic groups joined the Israelites (such as Rahab and her family). The Israelites also formed alliances with other ethnic groups. It is not ethnic cleansing, it is a religious cleansing. Some things matter so much that they cannot be contaminated by false ideas. It is also specific to a point in time for the Israelites, it is not offered as a pattern for human history.

Before modern critics dismiss this period of ancient Israel's history, let us remember events in the modern age. In 1945, the decision was taken to drop atomic weapons on Japan. Two hundred thousand people died as a direct result: men, women and children, along with all the animals. This destruction dwarfs anything that happened in ancient Israel. Was this justified? Christians will disagree but certainly those who have argued in its favour were moral people. The leaders and soldiers were not considered wicked as they weighed up the reasons for carrying out these bombings. Though realising that vast numbers of innocents would die along with any military target, they felt that there was a moral reason to go ahead. Even if we disagree with those decisions, we recognise that they were moral people with a justification for their actions.

How much more should we assume that God, the source of moral goodness, had reason for the more limited devastation of the Joshua conquests? And, as we look to the future, we know that God will yet bring the whole world into judgment. Not only is God able to take such decisions but He knows the thoughts of every heart and acts accordingly. Far from being an immoral book, the Old Testament provides a moral framework that enables us to know what is right and wrong, to condemn ethnic cleansing and to trust in God's final judgment (1 Cor. 4:5).

EIGHTEEN

Is God a Moral Monster?

The Bible has become a happy hunting ground for many who want to undermine faith in the God of the Bible.

After all, there are a lot of disturbing tales to be found there. Dwelling on stories like these, along with aspects of the legal code dealing with slavery, capital punishment and warfare, vocal critics argue that the God of the Bible is a monster. Richard Dawkins, in *The God Delusion*, describes the God he doesn't believe in as a 'control freak', an 'ethnic cleanser' and a 'malevolent bully'. Leslie Scrase, in *An Unbeliever's Guide to the Bible,* describes the God of the Old Testament as 'dishonest, capricious, cruel, jealous and violent.' Christopher Hitchens, in his provocatively titled *God is not Great*, claims that the Old Testament warrants slavery and ethnic cleansing.

The fact is that there are very difficult moral issues raised by what we read in the Old Testament. All sensitive Christians find problem passages. Critics catalogue a bewildering array of moral problems in the Old Testament. Stories of polygamy, genocide and slavery are highlighted in order to paint a picture of God as malevolent. What can we say in response? I think four points need to be clarified.

1. CREATION IDEAL

The Bible records history with a beginning, a middle and an end. In the beginning, creation is good. Men and women live in harmony. Creation has no hint of murder or slavery. These things follow the human rebellion against God. Sin disrupted creation and consequently we live in a world of evils and suffering. Some apparent evils have now become necessary – after all, not all wars are wrong, not every life taken is murder and punishment must involve some kind of pain or discomfort. Most of the Old Testament is concerned with the 'middle' of the story and that is not the creation ideal as it was in the beginning and as it will one day be when God makes all things new.

2. Ancient Near-Eastern context

God revealed Himself and created a nation in a real, historical context. It was a world with a slave-based economy, with city states often at war with each other, with polygamous marriages to ensure the continuation of family lines. The laws of the Old Testament regulate this behaviour. Slaves are to be treated humanely (Exod. 21:2-11). They are given rights and not seen as mere possessions. Hebrew slaves were able to buy their own freedom. Human trafficking is condemned (Exod. 21:16). In contrast to the law code of Babylon, Old Testament Israel was a light to the nations.

3. Biblical honesty

The Bible describes history and its participants, with flaws and failings exposed. As we read the Old Testament stories, we need to consider carefully what lesson we are actually being taught because a narrative may be descriptive but not necessarily prescriptive. It describes what happened but does not necessarily prescribe what should happen. This is important when we read the stories of the patriarchs and kings. They are flawed individuals. The Bible is brutally honest about their shortcomings. Far from being a matter of embarrassment, this helps to confirm the reliability of a text that does not gloss over the failure of its heroes.

4. THE BIBLE'S BIGGER STORY

The Old Testament law and narratives do not stand alone. Jesus is now our best interpreter of what we read. So the moral teaching of the Bible cannot be summarised by a brief and brutal quote taken out of context from the Old Testament. Slavery was permitted in Old Testament law. But it was regulated. And in the light of the whole Scriptural teaching, we find the reasons for its ultimate abolition (Eph. 6:9; Col. 4:1; Philem. 15-16 and Gal. 3:28). The Bible provided the moral impetus against slavery in the Roman Empire and against the slave trade in the New World.

But what of genocide or holy war in the book of Joshua? As we saw in the previous section, several things could be pointed out. The rhetoric of warfare in the ancient world did not always mean literal total destruction, even when events are described in such terms. We know that plenty of non-believers and pagan cities continued in the land after the time of Joshua. Who knows how many fled ahead of the Israelites from their cities to hide in the hills? Furthermore, the book of Joshua does not describe a genocide. It is not a race being destroyed, as in genocide, but a religious practice – which was often appalling and degrading. Those who repent are not destroyed but become part of Israel. It is not the racial group that is in view but their 'detestable practices'.

However, after all is said, we must still affirm that God brought judgment on the nations of Canaan. It is not our place in apologetics to sanitise the Bible. For some critics, this is enough to make God a moral monster. But the fact is that Jesus continued to affirm that God is a judge who will bring a future judgment on all peoples and all nations. God's judgment will be just. The list of Old Testament stories rejected by critics often leads to a similar dismissal of the New Testament teaching of Jesus on the existence of hell.

After all, what was the flood of Genesis or the conquest of Joshua if not a glimpse of future judgment? Hell does not demonstrate cruelty on God's part, but it does demonstrate His holiness and our accountability. Perhaps this is the real reason many people rail against the God of the Bible? It is not that they think He is a moral monster, but that they are afraid He is a moral judge, and that has implications for our behaviour now.

Part 4

Talk about the Church

NINETEEN

Where did the Church go wrong?

The figures are obvious. The church in the U.K. is in serious decline. In 1900, 55 per cent of children were in a Sunday school of some kind. In 2000, that number had dropped to 4 per cent. In addition, there has been a rapid growth in population, so that the number of churchgoing Christians, old or young, becomes ever more obviously a minority.

What is the cause of the decline? Many people imagine that it began after the Second World War. The baby-boom generation of the 1950s grew up without the traditional commitments of their parents. The 1960s cultural and sexual revolution saw an entire generation turn their backs on churchgoing. Therefore, the decline is often seen as a product of the past fifty years.

But the statistics do not bear out this interpretation. In his study (*The Empty Church Revisited*, 2003), Robin Gill demonstrates that the decline in U.K. churchgoing began long, long before the 1960s. In fact, the high-water mark for Anglican church attendance was 1851 and for free churches was 1880. Many of our chapel buildings were built since the decline set in and so many of the small, struggling chapels around the country have always been like that. There is something of a myth of chapels and churches bursting at the seams on a golden Sunday in 1900, but, even with the best estimate, 45 per cent of children were not in church that day.

Of course, for many evangelicals these statistics do not suggest that anything has gone wrong. They simply present the sorting of wheat from chaff. Nominal churchgoing has been in terminal decline. Who wants to spend time on a Sunday worshipping a god they don't believe exists? So the remaining small percentage represents true believers. This remnant has probably only ever been a minority in society at large. Whether we live in the medieval state of Christendom or the contemporary state of Secularism, true Christians have always been a small, and sometimes persecuted, minority.

But I think there is more that these figures can teach us than that. No doubt the large numbers who attended church in the early 1800s included many nominal believers, many forced to be there by families, landowners or cultural expectations.

Granted all this, something has happened to put off many people from bothering to have anything to do with the church or Christianity. So what else can explain the decline in church attendance in the U.K.?

Consider again that the high-water mark for church attendance was around 1851. What else has changed since then? What we call the Victorian age was part of a greater cultural revolution across Europe called the Enlightenment. This period witnessed great technological advance and intellectual progress. The deadweight of tradition, superstition and authoritarianism was being replaced by freedom of thought and enquiry. The Industrial Revolution benefited from the inventiveness of scientists. The political landscape of the West was changed by increasingly free, democratic progress. In biology, Charles Darwin in 1859 published *On the Origin of Species* which undermined the idea that human beings were the special creation of God.

In the area of theology, a new movement called Higher Criticism changed the way the Bible was read. Rather than being considered the inspired Word of God, the Bible was construed as a record of the slow, muddled progress of religious thought. The church itself began to peddle a theology of the Enlightenment devoid of miracles and wary of revelation. This was called liberal theology and it found a voice in pulpits across the land.

In the light of later church decline, we might as well say that the church hit its own self-destruct button. Christianity lost its authority and appeal as it lost confidence in its own foundations. Is it really a coincidence that the decline of churchgoing matched the rise of liberal theology? The church might try to offer moral teaching, psychological well-being, political reform or mystical experiences, but if the core of its teaching is not true then why not look elsewhere? As C.S. Lewis wrote in *Man or Rabbit?* (1946): 'If Christianity is untrue then no honest man will want to believe it, however helpful it might be; if it is true, every honest man will want to believe it, even if it gives him no help at all.'

So, if this diagnosis is correct, what should the church have been doing? Instead of retreating into an emotional or moral subjectivism, Christianity should have been giving an answer. This is 'apologetics'. Apologetics is derived from a Greek word meaning to give a 'word away' as we answer or reason with those who object to the Christian faith. At the church where I pastor and the theological college where I teach, I am convinced that every believer needs a robust confidence in their faith. Apologetics is not some specialised subject for Christians who wear anoraks. Every believer should want to present a credible case for historical Christianity in the modern world. The church of the nineteenth century gave up its own confidence; the pressing need of the contemporary church is to rediscover it.

TWENTY

Apologetics and preaching

When William Lane Craig gave a series of debates and lectures throughout the U.K. during October 2011, he ignited a lot of untapped enthusiasm for apologetics.

Craig is a significant apologist who has written numerous books and taken part in many debates. His presentation skills are highly effective and engaging. In the publicity for the tour, there is a quote from an 'irregular churchgoer' who heard Craig during his 2007 visit: 'Why isn't there more of this kind of thing being preached from church pulpits? If there were, I'd go more often and I'd stay awake during the sermon!' It's a good question. What is it that Craig is doing that is relevant to our pulpits?

Though I teach apologetics at a college and regularly preach at local churches, I rarely, if ever, use the word 'apologetics' in ministry. Why not? It's a technical word meaning 'to give a word back' or to defend the faith from objections. However, in contemporary use it seems to imply saying sorry. When it comes to our faith, Christians might rightly complain that they have nothing to apologise for!

But the fact that I do not use the word 'apologetics' does not mean that I do not use apologetics. The evidence for the Christian faith and the weakness of objections to our faith must be relevant to all Bible-based preaching. I am convinced that one of the weaknesses of the evangelical church is our general drift into devotional preaching.

What I mean by devotional preaching is the kind of sermon that (a) assumes the hearers are all believers and

(b) assumes the hearers are all convinced of the point being made. Therefore, all the preaching needs to do is to encourage fresh devotion to God on the part of those present. Devotional preaching can be warm, heartening and gentle. It can leave a congregation feeling satisfied and uplifted. But are those feelings based on fact? Or have underlying doubts and objections been temporarily swept aside? If so, might they not creep back into the light on Monday morning?

Preaching should convict the mind and move the heart. A devotional sermon can move the heart, but unless the mind is convicted what change can it really bring about?

When we stop to think about it, the Bible itself is apologetics. It is God's Word to a rebellious world. God speaks with clarity, gives reasons for faith, demolishes the alternatives and presents the case for His own authority. The Bible is not given as timeless poetry or heart-warming chicken soup for the soul. The Bible is a sustained word from God undermining all the rebellious attempts of the human race to sidestep His authority. The Bible is described as a double-edged sword – a weapon to cut through all the pretensions that set themselves up against God.

So how can we use the work of great apologists like William Lane Craig, or C.S. Lewis, Ravi Zacharias, Amy Orr-Ewing (the list gets rather long!) to benefit preaching? Not only can we do so, but we must do so. We must preach with the aim of clarifying truth, demolishing error and persuading hearts and minds. Let me suggest four ways of engaging apologetics in preaching.

1. Raise the Questions our World is Raising.

Ask questions like, 'Now you may be thinking, "How on earth can we be sure of this?"' Identify unsettling rumours: 'You may have heard that the four Gospels are not the only gospels written in the ancient world.' You will help a congregation see that your sermon is providing an answer to the questions that the world is asking. Just make sure that they genuinely are the questions people are asking and not the questions we wish they were!

2. Assume Little.

We are all aware that we live in an age of increasing biblical illiteracy. Is Robin Hood in the Bible? Did Jesus come before Noah? Was the Bible written in English? These are not daft questions any longer. Not only does apologetics help us defend the faith, it helps us to explain the faith.

3. Do not Belittle, Caricature or Dismiss Alternatives.

I'm tired of preachers rubbishing Nobel Laureate scientists or dismissing philosophers as fools. We may disagree with them, we may be hurt by their blasphemy, but we should always err on the side of respect and an honest attempt to take criticism seriously. Richard Dawkins may be irritating and arrogant, but as I said in the introduction: he can also be capable as a writer and has a great mind.

4. Give a Cogent Defence.

When marking essays I look not only for 'what' a student claims but 'why' they say so. What is their evidence? Do their conclusions follow logically from their research? When listening to a sermon, we should prize the same values of evidence and coherence. Why do you believe what you do? How does your point follow from the evidence you have given? Martyn Lloyd-Jones described preaching as 'logic on fire' and his sermons are great examples of cogent defence.

TWENTY-ONE

Where have all the men gone?

David Murrow, in his book *Why Men Hate Going to Church*, surveys a number of reasons why many churches have recorded a steep decline in male churchgoing. Across America and the United Kingdom, it seems that the proportion of female-to-male churchgoers is increasingly unbalanced. Obviously if men are disappearing, then the church will become increasingly oriented towards women. This will then make the church even less comfortable for men, and young boys will depart when they reach the age of maturity. Does this matter? It matters for a number of reasons, not least that many men become an unreached people group. Many wives are unable to share their faith with their partners and many children grow up associating church primarily with women. The statistics are even bleaker than this. Murrow shows that an increasingly female church is also a declining church. He writes, *'Once a church's adult attendance is 70 percent female, you can write its obituary.'* When a church becomes oriented towards women, even many women find it unattractive. On the other hand, a church that is reaching men will reach women too. There are some very obvious reasons for that!

So the next question is why do men hate going to church? Obviously it is a generalisation but there are many features of church life that make it particularly awkward for men. Apparent trivialities give men the subconscious message that they are not at home. A focus on flowers and pastel shades, singing songs which make Jesus sound like a romantic boyfriend, running family services which are really aimed only at children (and even the kids are given colouring-in sheets in case they get bored!). These are all features which remind many men that they are in alien territory. This problem is nothing new. Charles Spurgeon noted: 'There has got abroad a notion, somehow, that if you become a Christian you must sink your manliness and turn milksop.' The notion has not gone away!

I found Murrow's book very thought-provoking. We need to take a look at our religious language, architecture and pro-grammes. Have we become so used to a certain way of doing church that we do not even notice the subconscious message we are sending? But I think that there is a missing element in Murrow's book.

Christianity is not a myth or fairy tale. The gospel of Jesus Christ is the true story of a true Saviour who defeated death and conquered sin. Therefore, at the heart of church life is a true message that needs clear presentation and solid defence. We need to tackle the objections and rumours head-on. We provide arguments against unbelief and demonstrate Christianity is cast-iron truth. Debate and dispute can sometimes seem competitive and argumentative. Some Christians feel uncomfortable. Surely such direct engage-ment with unbelief is incompatible with the loving sensitivity of Jesus? However, the Jesus we read of in all the Gospels regularly engaged in confrontation and dispute (Matt. 21:23; Mark 7:1-23; Luke 11:53-54; John 8:13-14). The apostles continued this debate (Acts 6:9-10; Acts 9:29; Acts 18:28). The writings of early church history show us that the pastors, theologians and evangelists of that time were almost all engaged in debate and dialogue with non-Christian culture.

When did we come to think that a robust defence of the Christian faith is somehow incompatible with love and grace? Whenever that happened, the church became toothless! Why do men hate going to church? Perhaps one reason is that we are not giving a word back to those who ask us the reason for the hope we have within (1 Pet. 3:15). Apologetics is a necessary part of evangelism and church life. As we see with such leading examples as John Lennox, David Robertson, Ravi Zacharias and Mary Jo Sharp, when we confront unbelief with passion and conviction that the Bible is true we do something that engages men. And women.

TWENTY-TWO

A Symphony of Sorrowful Songs

As I have argued, apologetics really helps inform the way we preach, debate and evangelize. But what about when we come together to sing songs of praise and worship? Is apologetics relevant to our worship songs too?

The simple answer is that it must be. Paul tells us that when we come together and sing we are 'teaching' one another through those songs (Col. 3:16). Our songs help us understand God better, shape the attitudes of heart and mind, and teach others about what we believe. We think carefully about the case we make when preaching; should we not also think carefully about the case we make in our praise?

Don't worry. I am not going to spend time identifying lyrics I don't like! Nick Page, in his insightful book, *And Now Let's Move Into a Time of Nonsense* (Authentic, 2004), helpfully surveys the pitfalls of Christian songwriting. He expresses the frustration of many: 'Why, when the tunes are often so good, are the lyrics frequently so bad? Why are we content to stand there in church and sing stuff that really doesn't make any sense?' Here is a simple question to ask of any song we sing: is the content of what I am singing true?

I think this question moves beyond simply dismissing some songs as 'cheesy' or just romantic love songs with the name of Jesus thrown in. Those dismissals may be true but 'cheesiness' is a very subjective judgment (this coming from someone who still listens to the Carpenters...), and while many songs alarmingly make Jesus sound like a boyfriend, there is at least biblical precedent for using romantic imagery to describe our love for God. But do take a look at the top songs you sing on a Sunday and ask what reasons they give you to praise.

Some songs even revel in the idea that what we are doing is stupid; 'I feel like dancing / it's foolishness I know' – is that really going to persuade a sceptical member of our congregation to believe in Christ? When we read the story of David's dancing before the Lord, we also hear him give a good reason for his desire to dance (2 Sam. 6:21-22). There is a world of difference between appearing foolish and being foolish. David may have appeared foolish to Michal, just as we will appear foolish to some sceptics, but we do have reasons for what we believe and do.

Of course, nothing in what I have written implies that our music should be old-fashioned, set to dull tunes or lack devotional warmth. We need music that can carry the emotions and engage our hearts. We need to be culturally appropriate in our style today as Charles Wesley was in his day. But it is a false dichotomy to suggest that we have to choose between making a rational case for our faith and being in touch with our feelings. We do not make that split when presenting a sermon, so there is no reason why we should have to when singing a song.

Part 5

Talk about Culture

TWENTY-THREE

The Cautionary Tale of John Hick

Professor John Hick died in February 2012 at the age of 90. He leaves a legacy of over thirty books and countless articles. As a philosopher of religion, Hick has had great influence on many thinkers. He supervised evangelical Ph.D. students William Lane Craig and Harold Netland, along with those holding to his own more liberal ideas. Always clear and precise as a writer, his academic books are not difficult to read and his name will probably always be associated with what we call 'religious pluralism'.

Do all the major world religions provide pathways to the same God and salvation? As we have already seen, Hick thought so and sought to persuade others too.

But John Hick only gradually grew to hold these radical ideas and his story provides any apologist with a cautionary tale. In childhood, he attended a local Anglican church which he described as 'a matter of infinite boredom' and did not consider himself a Christian when he was eighteen years old. However, he describes having an evangelical conversion, particularly through the influence of the Christian Union at Hull University. This conversion influenced his decision to join the Quaker ambulance service as a pacifist during the Second World War and later to be ordained in what would become the United Reformed Church.

However, he served only briefly in local church ministry before entering a lifetime of academic scholarship. This brought to light the first shift in his theological thought. There was opposition when Hick took up a teaching post at

Princeton Theological Seminary in America during the 1960s. Technically, to be on the faculty one had to be in agreement with an orthodox confession of faith. Though Hick considered himself orthodox, he was unable to assent to doctrines like the Virgin birth or infallibility of the Bible. A drift away from evangelicalism was under way.

Hick returned to England to teach at Birmingham University, where he became involved in various interfaith groups with the laudable aim of promoting tolerance. He came to believe that Jesus was only one saviour figure among many and that Christianity had no unique standing as a path of salvation. This developing view culminated in a book he edited called *The Myth of God Incarnate* in 1977. Hick and his collaborators argued that Jesus was not to be considered literally unique, but only in some poetic or metaphorical sense. No longer was Christ a barrier or stumbling block to religious harmony. All religions might have their own myths, metaphors, poetry and saviours, but, behind them all, is the same God.

At least, that was Hick's position in the 1970s, but his thinking was drifting still further from the shore of orthodoxy. An obvious objection to his position would be to point out that not all religions assent to the existence of God. Zen Buddhism is generally considered atheist. And even many religions that do speak of a god do not mean a personal being. This observation led Hick to abandon the word 'God' in favour of what he called the Real or Ultimate Reality. This 'Real' was neither personal nor non-personal. Finding no suitable pronoun, Hick referred to the Real as 'He/She/It'.

Hick's final views were far more agnostic than Christian. His God had receded to a 'Real' beyond any understanding. Jesus Christ, the risen Saviour, had become only a poetic image to describe a man whose bones rotted in the earth long ago. Hick had sought to use philosophy as a tool to make Christianity credible. The rational 'faith' he ended up with was devoid of a personal God and empty of miracles. Instead of God-given revelation, Hick offered man-made speculation. Apologetics is the defence of the faith 'once for all entrusted to God's Holy people' (Jude 3). Hick's philosophical journey led him to discard the good deposit in favour of another gospel that really is no gospel at all (Gal. 1:7).

TWENTY-FOUR

C.S. Lewis and the Apologetics of Narnia

Read almost any book on the defence of the Christian faith and, somewhere, you are sure to find quotations from C.S. Lewis (including this one!).

The impact of this Christian scholar on popular apologetics is profound. One reason why Lewis is so quotable is that he had such a broad range of literary abilities. He wrote textbooks, science fiction, fantasy, allegory, poetry, letters and, of course, apologetics. With remarkable turns of phrase and metaphor, he makes complicated ideas seem simple and controversial arguments persuasive.

It is true that as a creative thinker he sometimes developed ideas that wandered into realms of speculation – though in most cases these seem to be suggestions along the way. Certainly, Lewis was no systematic theologian explaining the biblical basis for Christian doctrine. Rather, he was an academic who could popularise and defend important ideas. Many people came to enjoy the work of Lewis through *The Chronicles of Narnia* and they remain his best-selling work. He died in 1963 and, while some of his work will show signs of ageing over time, there is something forever fresh about the stories of a lion, a witch and a wardrobe.

The year 2012 marked the 60th anniversary of the publication of his most popular apologetic book, *Mere Christianity*. In 1941, Lewis began broadcasting a series of talks for BBC Radio which would continue until 1944. Though already published in shorter forms, his radio talks were combined into a single volume and published in 1952 as *Mere Christianity*. The title was borrowed from the Puritan, Richard Baxter, who described himself as 'a Christian, a meer Christian' (*sic*). Far from being a term of abuse, it describes the essential or 'pure' doctrines of the faith upon which, Lewis felt, our Christian witness should be focused.

As a book, *Mere Christianity* develops a compelling case for the faith and follows a pattern which can be found throughout Lewis's work. Firstly, he identifies a profound reason to believe in the supernatural. The existence of a moral law found the world over provides evidence for the existence of something outside of the natural world. Even though people may disagree on what counts as moral behaviour, there remains a universal conviction that there is such a thing as morality. Some of the first words young children use are to voice the complaint: 'That's not fair!' Somehow we seem to be born with a sense of right and wrong. This moral law is a signpost to the existence of a moral lawgiver who created our universe.

This kind of argument forms a pattern in Lewis's work. He identifies longings or beliefs that are already an important part of life and uses these as signposts to help us see a loving, holy, creator God to whom they point. *The Chronicles of Narnia* capture the sense that we have a longing for a world beyond this. Rather than dismissing such a longing as just wishful thinking, could it be an implication of God having placed eternity in our heart (Eccles. 3:11)? When the children hear the name of Aslan, they experience emotions which they can't explain: 'Lucy got the feeling you have when you wake up in the morning and realise that it is the beginning of the holidays or the beginning of summer.'

The success of Lewis's apologetics is the combination of two powerful weapons. In one hand there was a razor-sharp logic. But in the other there was a vivid imagination. The persuasive arguments of *Mere Christianity* and the enchanting stories of Narnia belong together as a great example of apologetics in action. Lewis could captivate heart and mind. It reminds us today that we must pay attention not only to what we are saying but how we say it. Lewis himself describes moving on to writing his imaginative fiction in the wake of *Mere Christianity* as a deliberate strategy. A philosophical or evangelistic tract may not find an open mind when read by a sceptic. But imaginative fiction works in a different way. Like watching dragons, the mind has its objections ready for anything it does not want to consider true. With bad experiences of church or Christians, our friends may be biased against anything we say. In 'Sometimes Fairy Stories May Say Best What's to Be Said', Lewis wrote: 'Supposing that by casting all these things into an imaginary world, stripping them of their stained-glass and Sunday School associations, one could make them for the first time appear in their real potency? Could one not thus steal past those watchful dragons? I thought one could.' We can see the legacy of Lewis as a twin strategy. He both showed that it would be good if Christianity were true and that Christianity really is true. He appealed both to the imagination and to reason.

TWENTY-FIVE

Francis Schaeffer and the New Europe

Isaac Newton famously said: 'If I have seen further it is by standing on the shoulders of giants.' Our fascination with novelty can lead many of us to end up reinventing the wheel or repeating the mistakes of the past. An awareness of those saints who have gone before us can help us see further and grow taller in our spiritual walk. One such giant was born just over a hundred years ago, in 1912, and became a pioneer missionary to Europe. Francis Schaeffer studied theology at Westminster Theological Seminary under another giant, Cornelius Van Til. He arrived in Switzerland in 1948 to church-plant in post-war Europe.

It was in Switzerland that Schaeffer experienced a crisis of faith and developed his own balanced approach to apologetics, learning the best from other masters, but integrating them with a genuine evangelist's heart. Schaeffer believed that the evangelical church was out of touch with contemporary culture. He had the foresight to recognize that cultural changes in central Europe, by then long established, were sweeping the entire Western world. Schaeffer identified a shift that happened in Europe when people gave up on a coherent world view of rational thought and abandoned values to being nothing more than matters of taste. Passing beyond a line of despair, people were led by their cultural elites into an era of anti-rational thought with no basis for values or meaning. This shift was on display in art galleries and cinemas across the Continent. As a missionary, Schaeffer saw clearly the failure of the church. Christians were not talking the language or understanding the world view of this new era. Continuing to preach and evangelize with the language and concepts of a previous generation, the church was failing to engage. He used the expression 'taking the roof off' to describe part of the task of evangelism. Rather than simply preaching the gospel, we need to take time to understand the pagan world views of contemporary culture and then demonstrate their weakness or incoherence (2 Cor. 10:3-5). This is not done out of spite or arrogance but out of love for those deluded by non-Christian world views.

Schaeffer died in 1984, and I first came across his work a few years later. I was studying Philosophy at Southampton University. As a Christian, I found it difficult to locate evangelical responses to some of the things I was being taught. But someone put me in touch with a little-known, local Christian ministry called L'Abri. I remember trying to describe it to my parents when I went to stay there and could not really explain what it was. A study centre? A retreat? A college? A community? A house of prayer? Whatever it was, I knew that it had been founded by Francis Schaeffer, and he was one of the few evangelical writers who cared about things like philosophy.

L'Abri (meaning 'the shelter') was established by Schaeffer in Switzerland and provided a place for people to think about and experience Christianity in community. L'Abri fellowships have sprung up all around the world but my own experience in England helped me understand the vision of Francis Schaeffer. Christianity was 'true truth' to be understood both as a philosophy and to be practised as a lifestyle. This holistic view of Christianity as a complete way of living inspired Schaeffer to engage with ethical issues like abortion and environmental change. Schaeffer taught extensively on Christian apologetics but never lost sight of the need for the church to live out this apologetic in community: 'After we have done our best to communicate to a lost world, still we must never forget that the final apologetic which Jesus gives is the observable love of true Christians for true Christians.' (*The Great Evangelical Disaster*)

I would maintain that the evangelical church must continue to value the work of Schaeffer. His main published books have been available as a rather intimidating multi-volume set, *The Complete Works*. If you want to know where to start, I would encourage anyone to read *Escape from Reason*, along with *Genesis in Space and Time*, and *Pollution and the Death of Man* in order to give a broad view of how this giant practised apologetics. Colin Duriez has recently written a fine biography, *Francis Schaeffer: An Authentic Life*. We are surrounded by a great cloud of witnesses as we run the race before us (Heb. 12:1), and Schaeffer is one of those witnesses who continues to give us encouragement!

TWENTY-SIX

Christianity's Critic

Born in 1955, he describes having a born-again, evangelical conversion as a teenager. He went to Moody Bible College, where he discovered a gift in reading the original languages of the Bible. This led him to further study at Wheaton College and postgraduate work at Princeton Theological Seminary. His doctoral work was under the supervision of Bruce Metzger, a name familiar to anyone who uses a Greek New Testament. Who am I describing? It might sound like the background of a Don Carson or a Craig Blomberg. It sounds like the credentials of a significant evangelical scholar. Sadly, this is the life story of a man who has become one of the most influential critics of biblical Christianity.

Bart Ehrman lost his faith during the course of his studies. His specialism today remains the text of the New Testament. But rather than confirming its accuracy, Ehrman has sold books by the thousands that pour scorn on its reliability. Anyone studying the reliability of the Bible today must reckon with Ehrman, and his views are becoming widely promoted in popular culture. Four of his books on New Testament studies have been in the *New York Times* best-seller lists. One of his most popular, *Misquoting Jesus*, has the subtitle 'The Story Behind Who Changed the Bible and Why.' Ehrman has done a great deal to undermine confidence that we can trust the Bible we use today as an accurate record of what was originally written. His oft-repeated claim is that 'There are more variations among our manuscripts than there are words in our New Testament.' This is the verdict of a New Testament scholar in a book that sold 100,000 copies in three months.

Ehrman is a competent scholar and he does know his facts. The data and evidence that he uses are well known. Anyone with a modern copy of the Greek New Testament with critical notes, such as the United Bible Societies edition, already has all the information at their fingertips. The serious question to ask is whether he is fair in his use of that evidence. For example, he conspiratorially informs us that no original manuscript of a New Testament book exists. We have nothing directly from the pen of Paul or John. What he neglects to mention is that no original manuscripts from any of the classics of the ancient world exist today. From the century before Christ, Julius Caesar wrote many books, about twelve of which we know today. Yet we do not have a single Latin word written in his hand. Everything we know of his writings comes from copies made in the Middle Ages. That original writings crumble and turn to dust is not a unique problem for Christians and their Scriptures.

The job of textual critics, Ehrman among them, is to reconstruct the original Greek text from the available manuscripts in order to establish what was originally written. Unlike those who read the works of Julius Caesar, the New Testament critic has many thousands of manuscripts to compare, some dating to within a century of the originals. More manuscripts continue to be found, including forty-seven Greek New Testament manuscripts discovered in Albania in 2008. Ehrman's estimate of 400,000 variations among manuscripts is probably correct. But this is indicative of the strength of New Testament study, not its weakness! Scientists need lots of data if they wish to make firm conclusions. The New Testament scholar has lots of data.

The vast majority of variations are minor matters – spellings and word order making up many of them. Far from leading scholars to scepticism about the original New Testament, most recognize this vast range of data to be a positive strength. It helps ensure that we can establish what the authors originally wrote to an extent that is simply impossible with the work of Julius Caesar. Yes, there are 400,000 variations. What needs to be emphasised is that most of them are minor.

However, there are some more important variations that Ehrman draws attention to. He uses these to imply that the New Testament we have is a serious distortion of what the authors originally said.

Ehrman refers to places where there are major additions to the New Testament and provides two 'examples'. The first is John 7:53–8:12, the story of the woman caught in adultery. The second is Mark 16:9-20, the longer ending of Mark's Gospel. Ehrman provides reasons why these passages probably did not belong to the original Gospels. He offers these as two 'examples' of the corruption of the manuscript and says that they might be 'surprising' to readers of the New Testament (Ehrman, *Whose Word Is It?*). The impression is given that these are somehow sensational discoveries that rock our faith. The fact is that anyone who reads the Gospels in any contemporary translation will have noticed them. The NIV marks both passages off from their gospel settings with a clear explanation of the problem. These are well-known passages that were probably not original to John or Mark.

However, by describing these as 'examples', Ehrman insinuates that the problem is greater than it really is. He implies there are many more like them. Having described them at length, he observes, 'Most of the changes [to the Bible] are not of this magnitude.' (Ehrman, *Whose Word Is It?*,

p. 69). What he should have written is *'no'* other changes are of this magnitude! He has picked two, obvious, well-known additions to the text and insinuated that there are others of this length when nothing can be further from the truth. After these obvious examples, most of the 400,000 variations often cited are matters of minor concern. New Testament scholar Arthur G. Patzia writes, 'Unintentional errors account for about 95 percent of the variants that are found in the New Testament.' (Patzia, *The Making of the New Testament*). Unintentional errors are matters like obvious slips of the pen. The remaining five per cent are examples like Mark 1:41 where we cannot be sure if the author originally described Jesus as having 'compassion', or, as Ehrman prefers, being 'angry'. The difference is not dramatic, though it provides fuel for a major book by Ehrman in which he argues the early church distorted their portrait of Christ.

Long ago, C.S. Lewis commented on the work of biblical scholars. He was disturbed that in their painstaking attempts to reconstruct a different view of Christianity by reading between the lines, 'they claim to see fern-seed and can't see an elephant ten yards away in broad daylight.' (C.S. Lewis, *Fern-Seed and Elephants*, p. 111). Ehrman provides a good discussion of the fern-seed of Mark 1:41. But he misses the elephant in the room. What other ancient writings are we able to debate over in such detail and present a case for the authenticity of a single word? There is a lot less to do in the textual studies departments of the ancient classics because there is a lot less material to study. The vast bulk of New Testament material provides data that allows us to make confident claims regarding the Scriptures as originally given.

Lewis originally wrote his essay in order to point out a problem in the clergy: 'Once the layman was anxious to hide the fact that he believed so much less than the vicar: he now tends to hide the fact that he believes so much more. Missionary to priests of one's own church is an embarrassing role; though I have a horrid feeling that if such mission work is not soon undertaken the future history of the Church of England is likely to be short.' (C.S. Lewis, *Fern-Seed and Elephants*, p. 125). Lewis's concerns for the clergy turned out to be almost prophetic. Might we not have the same concern for biblical criticism? The scholars who cannot see that they are involved in a rich discipline with plenty of data, providing a good case for the original form of the Bible, are probably only demolishing the foundations of their own profession. The real fruit of textual criticism has been greater confidence in the reliability of the Bible, not less! For a detailed response to Ehrman's work, see Timothy Paul Jones, *Misquoting Truth* (IVP, 2007).

TWENTY-SEVEN

Hollywood Apologetics

These days it is quite common to watch a film clip as part of a sermon or Bible study. It may be a famous scene from a classic movie, or a YouTube download of an advert that has gone viral. For many Bible teachers, it is second nature to integrate technology and multimedia with their message. Often this takes the form of illustration. Two thousand years ago, Jesus pointed to a farmer out sowing seed and builders at work on the lakeside as illustrations of His theological message. Multimedia is nothing new. Jeremiah was at least as adept at presenting a multimedia message as any tech-savvy youth worker today (Jer. 28:10-11).

However, using film as illustration stops short of a more important task facing the church. The reality is that many people are digesting the messages and discovering their ethics in the movies they watch. Novels, plays and songs have always had this power. Even if the message is subtle, they do more than entertain. They teach, or preach, ideas and values to those who listen. In contemporary society, the most powerful media must be the films and programmes watched on television, cinema and the Internet. Some of these values are good, and even biblical teachings are conveyed this way. But plenty of false ideas and destructive values are promoted in this form.

Rather than simply using film as a form of illustration for the gospel, the church must engage with the message of the movies. What world views lie behind the stories they tell?

What lifestyle is encouraged or promoted? In what ways do these films undermine or uphold the Bible?

When Peter challenges us to defend our faith against the critics, he tells us to give an answer to 'everyone who asks you to give the reason for the hope that you have' (1 Pet. 3:15). A key point in this verse is sometimes missed. We are supposed to be answering the questions people are actually asking, not questions we wish they would ask! The verse challenges us to ask ourselves whether we are living provocative lives. Do our church communities and our personal walk with the Lord provoke people to ask us questions? They should!

We can also discover the questions people are asking through media. In what way is Christianity or the supernatural being portrayed in the media? What questions are films asking and what misleading answers might they be giving? Some films offer a bleak and nihilistic world view (*Crimes and Misdemeanors* or *Fight Club*) while others delight in the ambiguity of our postmodern age (*Life of Pi*). There are films that pose alternative accounts of creation (*Prometheus*) or life after death (*What Dreams May Come*). Some films clearly aim to take a swipe at Christianity (*The Invention of Lying* or *Life of Brian*) but others can be allies in apologetics. The search for forgiveness (*Atonement*) or the problem of evil (*Tree of Life*) all have powerful movie treatments. Surprisingly, the weaker movies can be those with the more direct connection to Bible content, as the history gets distorted to fit a modern message. Even so, at least such films can ignite interest in what the Bible does say (*Noah* [2014] and *The Passion of the Christ* [2004]).

Watching a film with a friend can be a significant opportunity to share our faith and discuss the gospel. Some church groups will even choose to watch a film together as a prelude to an evangelistic talk or discussion. But everyone who preaches needs to be aware of the cultural questions around us. Some preachers are well equipped to engage with the questions of a previous generation. Apologetics demands that we are equipped to engage with the questions of today! As Paul carefully observed the culture of Athens, we need to do the same today (Acts 17:22-23).

CONCLUSION

This book may be over, but its contents are not! The need to defend and confirm the faith (Phil. 1:7) will always be a relevant task when there are objections and questions to address. We face a moving target. As questions change and problems arise, Christians must keep thinking on their feet and responding to the challenge of the moment.

If you are not yet a Christian and read this book out of interest then it would not surprise me that you have questions untouched by this volume. I would only encourage you to continue your honest investigation. There are many more books and resources (see the further reading list!) to guide your journey. But the best environment to get answers to your questions is to experience Christian community. Find a church where there are people who have sincere faith, love the Bible and speak of Jesus. Watch them and talk to them. What has transformed their lives? How do they deal with their questions? How do you explain their faith?

If you are a Christian and want to help unbelieving friends with their honest doubts then I would encourage you to see this book as an example. Apologetics is not the discipline of learning pat answers for difficult questions. It is not memorising the final word to use in any and every conversation. Apologetics requires good listening. Francis Schaeffer explained his approach to evangelism this way, 'If I have only an hour with someone, I will spend the first 55 minutes asking questions and finding out what is troubling their heart and mind, then the last 5 minutes I will share something of the truth.' With 55 minutes of questions and listening we are better prepared to give our word back. It will be the right word for the right person at the right moment!

But let us not be naïve. There are more reasons to believe or not believe than those we put into words. This is evident to me when many atheists honestly admit that they would refuse to believe in the resurrection of Christ no matter what evidence is placed before them. It is not simply a matter of logic, history and argument. As Blaise Pascal said 'The heart has its reasons of which reason knows nothing. We feel it in a thousand things.' Clearly this is true of faith where our beliefs, while not irrational, move beyond what could merely be a logical proof. But the comment is also true for the non-believer. There may be many reasons why they refuse to believe the evidence: bad experiences of church, a lifetime of habits, refusal to admit defeat.

Such a condition is illustrated so clearly in the lives of two of the twentieth centuries greatest atheists. A. J. Ayer (1910–1989), Oxford University Philosopher, had a remarkable experience at the end of his life. In 1988 he recovered from several minutes of having been pronounced clinically dead, in which he believed that he encountered the creator of the universe. He wrote an article about it describing the experience under the title 'What I saw when I was Dead'. The doctor said that after his recovery, Ayer had told him, 'I saw a Divine being. I'm afraid I'm going to have to revise all my books and opinions.' Under pressure from hostile colleagues, the only thing Ayer revised was the article itself which he diluted in order to maintain that he continued to doubt that there was a God or any life after death. Even that final experience did not seem enough to overturn his deep seated opposition to God.

Another great atheist of the twentieth century was Anthony Flew (1923–2010). Flew was also trained at Oxford and could count C.S. Lewis among his teachers. An ardent atheist throughout his working life, Flew had engaged in a number of debates on the resurrection and existence of God. Towards the end of his life he changed his mind.

Flew had always accepted the good historic credentials for much of the Christian faith. In a 2004 debate with Gary Habermas he declared, 'The evidence for the resurrection is better than for claimed miracles in any other religion. It's outstandingly different in quality and quantity.' Flew was impressed by the newly emerging Intelligent Design movement and his position changed from atheist to theist. We do not know if Flew finally came to believe in Jesus Christ as his personal saviour, but he certainly demonstrated the integrity of a man who could go where the evidence would take him.

A.J. Ayer and Anthony Flew responded to the evidence they encountered in different ways. That is true for you and for your friends. The same argument, sermon or idea can see one converted to Christ and the other confirmed in their scepticism. What is the difference? The heart knows things that reason does not. But, in every case, one thing is clear. Words matter. Arguments help. It may be a life long conversation, but the opportunity for faith remains open until we draw out final breath (Heb. 9:6). We must keep talking, asking, answering, thinking and back chatting because while there is life there is opportunity for faith.

GOING FURTHER

An Apologetics Reading List

1. ENGAGING WITH APOLOGETICS

Craig, William Lane, *On Guard: Defending Your Faith with Reason and Precision*, Ontario: David C. Cook, 2010

McGrath, Alister E., *Mere Apologetics: How to Help Seekers & Sceptics Find Faith*, Grand Rapids: Baker Books, 2012

Sinkinson, Chris, *Confident Christianity: Conversations that lead to the Cross*, Nottingham: IVP, 2012

Sire, James W., *Why Good Arguments often fail: Making a More Persuasive Case for Christ*, Leicester: IVP, 2006

2. ENGAGING WITH HISTORY

Collins, John J. and Craig A. Evans (eds.), *Christian Beginnings and the Dead Sea Scrolls*, Grand Rapids: Baker Books, 2006

Collins, Steven and Latayne C. Scott, *Discovering the City of Sodom*, New York: Howard Books, 2013

Jones, Timothy Paul, *Misquoting Truth*, Downers Grove: IVP, 2007

Moore, James, *The Darwin Legend*, Grand Rapids: Baker, 1994

Ritmeyer, Leen, *The Quest: Revealing the Temple Mount in Jerusalem*, Jerusalem: Carta, 2006

Sinkinson, Chris, *Time Travel to the Old Testament*, Nottingham: IVP, 2013

3. ENGAGING WITH BIG QUESTIONS

Copan, Paul, *Is God a Moral Monster?* Grand Rapids: Baker Books, 2011

Keller, Timothy, *The Reason for God: Belief in an Age of Scepticism*, London: Hodder & Stoughton, 2008

Robertson, David, *The Dawkins Letters*, Ross-shire: Christian Focus, 2007

Wright, Christopher J. H., *The God I Don't Understand: Reflections on Tough Questions of Faith*, Grand Rapids: Zondervan, 2008

Zacharias, Ravi and Norman Geisler (eds.), *Who Made God? And Answers to over 100 other Tough Questions of Faith*, Grand Rapids: Zondervan, 2003

4. Engaging with the Church

Altrock, Chris, *Preaching to Pluralists: How to Proclaim Christ in a Postmodern Age*, Missouri: Chalice Press, 1998

Downes, Martin, *Risking the Truth: Handling Error in the Church*, Ross-shire: Christian Focus, 2009

Murrow, David, *Why Men Hate Going to Church*, Nashville: Thomas Nelson, 2010

Page, Nick, *And Now Let's Move into a Time of Nonsense: Why Worship Songs are failing the Church*, Carlisle: Authentic, 2004

5. Engaging with Culture

Godawa, Brian, *Hollywood Worldviews: Watching Films with Wisdom & Discernment*, Downers Grove: IVP, 2009

Horner, Grant, *Meaning at the Movies: Becoming a Discerning Viewer*, Wheaton: Crossway, 2010

Johnston, Robert K., *Reel Spirituality: Theology and Film in Dialogue*, Grand Rapids: Baker, 2006

Pollard, Nick, *Evangelism Made Slightly Less Difficult*, Leicester: IVP, 1997

Turnau, Ted, *Popologetics: Popular Culture in Christian Perspective*, Phillipsburg: P&R, 2012

Watkins, Tony, *Focus: The Art and Soul of Cinema*, Southampton: Damaris Publishing, 2007

Christian Focus Publications

Our mission statement –

STAYING FAITHFUL

In dependence upon God we seek to impact the world through literature faithful to His infallible Word, the Bible. Our aim is to ensure that the Lord Jesus Christ is presented as the only hope to obtain forgiveness of sin, live a useful life and look forward to heaven with Him.

Our books are published in four imprints:

CHRISTIAN
FOCUS

CHRISTIAN
HERITAGE

Popular works including biographies, commentaries, basic doctrine and Christian living.

Books representing some of the best material from the rich heritage of the church.

MENTOR

CF4•K

Books written at a level suitable for Bible College and seminary students, pastors, and other serious readers. The imprint includes commentaries, doctrinal studies, examination of current issues and church history.

Children's books for quality Bible teaching and for all age groups: Sunday school curriculum, puzzle and activity books; personal and family devotional titles, biographies and inspirational stories – because you are never too young to know Jesus!

Christian Focus Publications Ltd,
Geanies House, Fearn, Ross-shire,
IV20 1TW, Scotland, United Kingdom.
www.christianfocus.com